중학 내신만점

영문법 쏙쏙·영어 쑥쑥

하늘편

저자 동영상 강의 예정
www.seeenglish.com

시잉글리쉬
www.seeenglish.com

중학 내신만점
영문법 쏙쏙 · 영어 쑥쑥 (하늘편)

초판 발행: 2016년 1.1일

지은이 · 손 창 연
펴낸이 · 손 창 연
표지디자인 · 전 철 규
내지디자인 · 필커뮤니케이션
인쇄 · 송죽문화사
펴낸곳 · **시잉글리쉬**
서울 서초구 양재동 106-6 정오 B/D 402호(우 137-891)
Tel: [02] 573-3581
등록번호 제 22- 2733호
Homepage: **www.seeenglish.com**

ISBN:

정가: 13,000원

들어가는 _ 말

무엇이든 기본이 중요하다.
영어를 가르치기 시작한지도 20여년이 넘었다. 그 동안 중고생들과 대학생 및 성인 등에게 TOEFL, TOEIC, 편입영어, 수능, 중고생 내신 등을 가르치면서 느낀 점은 역시 '기본이 중요하다'라는 것이다. 특히 영어문법은 처음 시작할 때 제대로 배워야 한다는 생각이다.

이 책은 영어를 학습하는 중학생을 위한 책이다. 상위권 초등 5,6학년에게도 어렵지 않다. 학교 영어수업을 이해하고 영어시험에 빈틈없이 준비할 수 있도록 했다. 또한 영어의 기본을 확실하게 하고자 했다.

모든 공부나 세상의 일들이 그렇듯이 영어라는 바다에 나가 자유롭게 항해하기 위해서는 영어단어 하나하나를 꼼꼼히 읽히고, 아주 기초적인 문장에 대한 이치를 정확하게 읽혔을 때, 풍랑에도 안전하게 항해 할 수 있는 진정한 영어실력을 갖출 수 있다.

로마가 하루 아침에 이루어 지지 않았듯이(Rome wasn't built in a day.) 영어도 하루 아침에 이루어 질 수 있는 것이 아니다. 긴 시간동안 끊임없는 암기와 이해, 반복적인 학습이 필요하다.

이 책에서 제시하는 내용을 꼼꼼히 잘 읽히고 문제를 풀어나가다 보면, 자기도 모르는 사이 영어실력이 부쩍 늘었다는 것을 알게 될 것이다.

끝으로 이 책으로 학습하는 모든 학생들이 단 한번 밖에 없는 인생에서 자신의 꿈을 이루고, 인류의 평화와 자유, 그리고 민주주의를 위해 각각의 그릇에 맞는 기여를 하길 기원한다.

2016년 1월 1일
저자 손 창 연

쫄지 말고 열공 ^^

[이 책을 이렇게 공부하자.]

◆ 학습자의 수준에 따라 다르겠지만 작은 챕터는 하루에 하나 긴 챕터는 2~3일에 정복해보자.

◆ 각 챕터의 핵심개념을 정확히 이해 한다. 또 해당 예문을 꼼꼼히 익힌다.

◆ '**확인문제**'를 통하여 핵심개념을 심화하고 순발력을 강화한다. '**확인문제**' 문장들도 문제의 답을 찾는데 그치지 않고 각각 해석도 해본다. 언어는 의미파악이 주요 목적이고 문법은 그 의미를 정확하게 하기 위함이다.

◆ '**Reading in Grammar**'에서 문제를 풀면서 독해속에서 활용을 해본다.

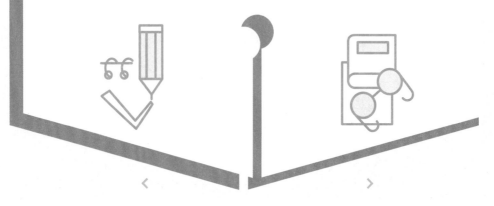

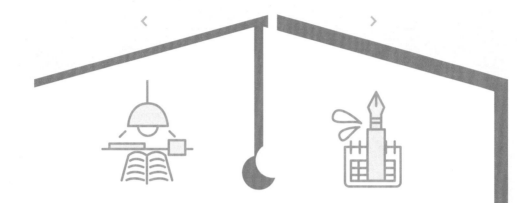

◆ **'중간·기말고사 내신만점대비문제'**를 풀면서 다시 한번 보다 치밀

하게 학습한다.

◆ **별책 단어책**의 단원별 단어들을 꼼꼼히 학습하자. 영어학습에서 빼

놓을 수 없는 것이 어휘이다. 아무리 설계가 좋고 높은 건물일지라도

벽돌 등 하나하나의 자재 없이 건물은 완성 될 수 없기 때문이다.

◆ 마지막으로 최고의 학습법이자 성공의 팁은 **끈기**다.

기억하자!

[느리지만 꾸준히만 한다면 이길 수 있다.]

Slow but steady wins the race.

이 책의 _ **구성**

Structure

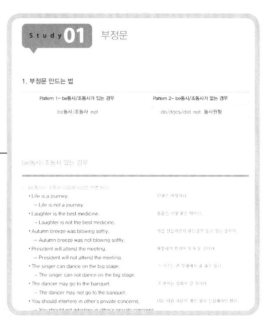

문법핵심 정리와 해설

문법을 이해하기 위한 핵심적인
내용을 예문과 함께 설명했다.

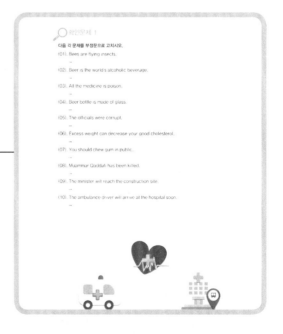

확인문제

문법핵심내용을 확인하고 활용하도록
핵심내용을 문제로 풀어보도록 했다.

Grammar in Reading

배운 내용을 쉬운 지문의 독해속에서
도 활용할 수 있도록 어법상 맞지 않는
것을 찾는 문장 등의 문법문제를 출제
했다.

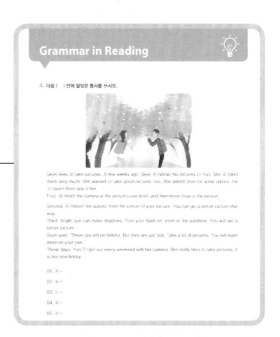

중간 · 기말고사
내신만점대비문제

각 단원에서 배운 문법내용을 다시
한번 점검하고 영작 등으로 응용할 수
있도록 했다.

이를 통해 학교 내신시험에 철저히
대비할 수 있는 힘을 기르도록 했다.

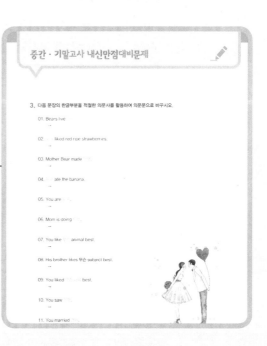

이 책의 _ **차례**

중학내신만점 영문법 쏙쏙 · 영어 쑥쑥   하늘편

 부록

Solution (정답과 해설)

이 책의 _ **차례**

별 책

중학내신만점
영문법 쏙쏙 · 영어 쑥쑥 [땅편]

땅 편

중학내신만점
영문법 쏙쏙 · 영어 쑥쑥 [바다편]

Prestudy
말들의 종류(품사)와 말들의 역할(성분)

말들의 종류(품사)

명사, 대명사, 동사, 형용사
부사, 접속사, 전치사, 감탄사

말들의 역할(성분)

주어, 주어의 동사, 목적어,
보충어(주어보충어, 목적어보충어) ,
수식어구, 동격 등

동물의 종류에는 사자, 호랑이, 닭, 개, 돼지 등이 있는 것 처럼 말의 종류에는 명사(대명사), 동사, 형용사, 부사, 전치사, 접속사 등이 있다.

그들이 동물의 왕국을 만든다면 대장과 왕과 장관, 중간간부, 졸병 등으로 구성 될 것이다. 문장에서 바로 이러한 역할을 하는 것이 주어, 주어의 동사, 목적어, 보충어, 수식어구 등이다.

【 동물들 】

【 동물의 왕국 】

Prestudy I : 말들의 종류(품사)

2개 핵심 품사(명사와 동사)

1. 명사

사람이나 사물 등 세상의 모든 것들의 이름을 말하는 말이다. 눈에 보이지 않는 추상적인 것들의 이름도 명사다.

(1). 명사의 뜻

사람, 생물 및 무생물의 사물, 추상적인 개념 등 모든 이름을 말한다.

① 사람; Mallory, Jared, Hector, mom, dad, a painter, a teacher, etc.

② 사물; a school, a building, a picture, a photo, a clock, a computer, a factory, a violin, a ball, a wallet, etc.

③ 동물: a snake, a pig, a chicken, a duck, a dog, etc.

④ 식물: a rose, a pine tree, a flower, a lily, bean, coffee, etc.

⑤ 무생물: air, stone, water, wood, iron, etc.

⑥ 학문이름: physical education, music, math, chemistry, biology, etc.

⑦ 스포츠명: baseball, soccer, etc.

⑧ 추상적 개념: freedom, peace, birth, history, test, entrance, love, war, etc.

(2). 명사의 문장에서의 역할– 문장에서 주어, 목적어, 보충어, 전치사 뒤에 사용한다.

① 주어

- The moon is bright.   달이 밝다.

② 목적어

- People see the moon on the Chuseok.   사람들은 추석에 달을 본다.

③ 보충어

- That is your car.   저것이 너의 차다.

cf) 대명사– 명사를 대신해 쓰는 말로 명사처럼 주어. 목적어. 보충어 자리 등에서 쓰인다. 명사의 일종이라고 생각해도 무방하겠다.

I, we, it, this, that, one, those 등

- We are a world. <주어>   우리는 하나의 세계다.
- The people follow him. <목적어>   국민들은 그를 따른다.
- That car is mine. <보충어>   저 차는 나의 것이다.

2. 동사

움직임이나 상태를 나타내는 말이다. 우리 말로 '~~다'로 끝나는 말을 일컫는다. 문장에서 주어의 동사(보통 주어뒤) 자리에서 사용된다.

(1). 동작: 움직임이 있는 말

run, swim, manage, build, cut, buy, take, teach, etc.

- The children run on the field.   아이들이 운동장에서 달린다.
- Mom buys many things every week.   엄마는 많은 것들을 산다.

(2). 상태: 움직임이 없는 말

like, lose, have, hate, etc.

- Sons and daughters like dad and mom.   아들과 딸들은 아빠와 엄마를 사랑한다.

B 2개 핵심품사인 명사와 동사를 각각 꾸며주는 형용사와 부사

1. 명사 꾸며주는 형용사

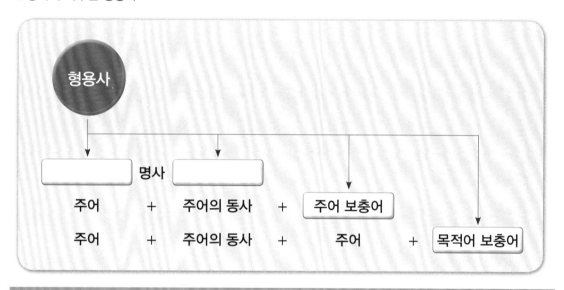

성질이나 상태, 크기, 색깔이나 재료, 모양 등을 나타내는 말이다.

- **성질:** angry, soft, tough, cool, hot, warm, cold, etc.
- **상태:** silent, motionless, lonely, shining, rough, slippery, smooth, etc.
- **재료:** wooden, etc.
- **색깔:** red, yellow, black, white, blue, green, etc.
- **크기:** large, small, tall, short, long, etc.

형용사는 문장에서 명사의 앞과 뒤, 주어보충어, 목적어 보충어 자리에서 명사를 꾸며주며 지원한다.

① **명사 앞**

- The short boy has many girl friends.   그 키 작은 소년은 많은 여자 친구가 있다.

② **(대)명사 뒤**

- Someone strange visited me.   낯선 어떤 사람이 나를 방문했다.

③ **주어 보충어**

- The train is very long.   그 열차는 매우 길다.

④ 목적어 보충어
- My parents always keep me happy. 나의 부모는 항상 나를 행복하게 유지한다.

2. 동사, 형용사, 다른 부사, 문장전체 꾸며주는 부사

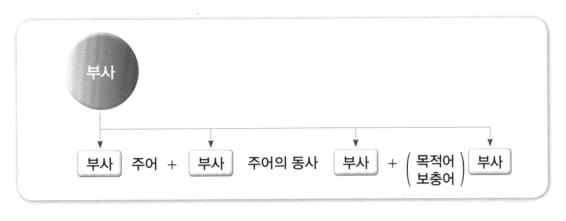

동사 앞뒤에서 동사를 꾸며주는 말이다. 또 형용사나 다른 부사, 문장전체의 앞뒤에서 형용사, 다른 부사, 문장전체를 꾸며 주며 후원한다.

(1). 부사의 뜻
장소, 때, 방법, 정도 등을 나타내는 말이다.

- 장소: here, there, inside, etc.
- 때 : then, once, etc.
- 방법: slowly, fluently, fast, etc.
- 정도: very, really, so, etc.
- 기타: merrily, happily, sadly, etc.

(2). 부사의 역할

① 동사를 꾸며준다.
- He always drives to work. 그는 항상 운전하여 일하러 간다.
- The runner runs fast. 그 런너는 빠르게 달린다.

② 형용사를 꾸며준다.
- The bridge is very long. 그 다리는 매우 길다.

③. 다른 부사를 꾸며준다.
- The man turned very swiftly to the right. 그 남자는 매우 신속하게 오른 쪽으로 돌았다.

④ 문장전체를 꾸며준다.
- Finally, the man didn't die. 마침내 그 남자는 죽지 않았다.

 명사를 연결하는 전치사와
기본문장(주어+동사~)를 연결하는 접속사

1. 명사 앞에 오는 전치사

(1). 전치사의 뜻

명사 앞에 놓는 말로 명사의 자리를 만들어 명사를 연결한다.

at, on, in, for, with, of, to, along, between, across, around, etc.

(2). 전치사의 역할

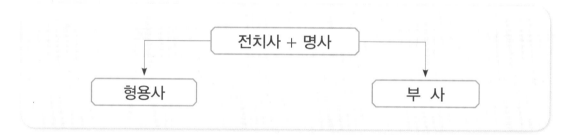

① (대)명사를 꾸며주는 형용사로 사용

• <u>The books</u> in the room are from my friend.

방안에 있는 책들은 나의 친구로 부터 온 것이다.

• Alice will take <u>some</u> of the books.

Alice가 그 책들 중 얼마간을 가져 갈 것이다.

② 동사, 형용사, 문장전체 등을 꾸며주는 부사로 사용

• 동사수식

My friends <u>live</u> in the village.

내 친구들이 그 마을에서 산다.

• 형용사 수식

The bucket is <u>full</u> of water.

그 양동이는 물로 가득 찼다.

• 문장전체수식

<u>I usually go skiing</u> in February.

나는 보통 2월에 스키 타러 간다.

2. 두개의 절(주어+동사~)를 연결하는 접속사

(1). 접속사의 뜻
문장의 기본인 '주어+동사~'형태의 두 개의 절을 연결한다.

(2). 접속사의 역할
접속사로 연결된 '접속사+주어+동사'는 명사나 형용사, 부사로 역할하는 경우가 많다.

① 명사절을 연결하는 접속사 ;

that, whether, who, which, when, where, what, etc.
- I think that you are right.　　　　　　　　　　나는 네가 옳다고 생각한다.

② 형용사절을 연결하는 접속사;

who, whose, whom, which, when, where, why, etc.
- The man who is singing on the stage is my husband.　　무대에서 노래하고 있는 여자는 내남편이다.

③ 부사절을 연결하는 접속사;

because, if, unless, when, though, although, where, as, while, that, etc.
- If you love me, set me free.　　　　　　　　네가 나를 사랑한다면 나를 자유롭게 해주세요.

cf) and, or, nor 등으로 연결된 절은 명사절, 형용사절, 부사절 역할이 아니고 독자적인 절이다.

- I want coffee, and my son wants cocoa.　　　나는 커피를 원하고 나의 아들은 코코아를 원한다.

Prestudy Ⅱ : 말들의 문장에서의 역할(성분)

필수 요소들 ＋ **부가 요소들**

문장은 문장에서 꼭 필요한 필수요소들과 부가적인 요소들로 구성되어 있다.

A 필수 요소들

주 어	주어의 동사	목 적 어	보(충)어	
			주어보충어	목적어보충어

1. 주어

문장에서 가장 중요한 요소로 동사의 행위자를 말한다. 우리말로 '~은, 는, 이, 가' 등으로 해석한다.

① 주어자리에는 명사가 사용할 수 있다.

- The sun disappeared.　　　　　　　　　　태양이 사라졌다.
- Robert is her brother.　　　　　　　　　로버트는 그녀의 오빠이다.
- Music is a worldwide language.　　　　음악은 세계적인 언어다.

또 명사의 친구들이 주어가 될 수 있다. 명사의 친구들에는 '대명사', 'to 동사원형', '동사원형ing', 명사절(that 주어+동사, whether/if 주어+동사, 의문사 주어+동사) 등이 쓰일 수 있다.

② 대명사

- He is a good pianist.　　　　　　　　　그는 훌륭한 피아니스트이다.
- You are my true friend.　　　　　　　　너는 나의 진정한 친구다.

③ 'to 동사원형'

- To love others is a basic emotion.　　　다른 사람들을 사랑하는 것은 기본적인 감정이다.

④ 동사원형ing

- Helping the poor is our duty.　　　　　가난한 사람을 돕는 것은 우리 의무다.

⑤ 명사절: that 주어+동사, whether/if 주어+동사, 의문사 주어+동사, what 주어+동사 등

- That he is diligent is certain.　　　　　그가 근면하다는 것은 확실하다.
- Whether she likes me or not is no concern of mine.　　그녀가 나를 좋아 하든 말든 나의 관심이 아니다.
- How he got the money is still a mystery.　　그가 어떻게 그 돈을 벌었는가는 여전히 수수께끼다.

2. (주어의) 동사

문장에서 주어의 동작이나 상태를 표현하는 말을 말한다. 동사만이 '주어의 동사'로 사용할 수 있다. 보통은 주어 뒤에 온다.

- The monster drinks coffee.
- Nina begins her work at 8;00.
- Brian plays soccer on Sundays.

그 괴물은 커피를 마신다.
나나는 그녀의 일을 8시에 시작한다.
브라이언은 일요일에 축구를 한다.

하지만 동사가 성격을 바꾼 'to 동사원형', '동사원형ing', 'p.p-과거분사'는 동사가 아니다. 즉 주어의 동사가 아니므로 문장이 성립될 수 없다.

- The monster to drink coffee. (×)
- Nina beginning her work at 8;00. (×)
- The driver begun his work. (×)

3. 목적어

문장에서 동사의 대상을 말한다. 우리말로 '~을, 를' 등으로 해석한다.

① 목적어자리에는 명사가 사용될 수 있다.
- My brother plays the guitar.   나의 형은 기타를 연주한다.
- The woman does aerobics.   그 여자는 에어로빅을 한다.
- Sue speaks five languages.   Sue는 5개 언어를 말한다.
- Donna lost the bike last week.   도나는 지난주 그 자전거를 잃어버렸다.
- Edison invented the light bulb.   에디슨은 전구를 발견했다.

또 명사의 친구들이 목적어가 될 수 있다. 명사의 친구들에는 '대명사', 'to 동사원형', '동사원형ing', 명사절(that 주어+동사, whether/if 주어+동사, 의문사 주어+동사)등이 쓰일 수 있다.

② 대명사
- The musician loves her.   그 음악가는 그녀를 사랑한다.
- People met them on the road.   사람들은 길에서 그들을 만났다.

③ to 동사원형
- They want to watch TV.   그들은 TV를 보기를 원한다.
- Mozart started to play the piano.   모짜르트는 피아노를 치기 시작했다.

④ 동사원형ing
- Babra enjoys playing the piano.   바브라는 피아노를 연주하는 것을 즐긴다.

⑤ 명사절: that 주어+동사, whether/if 주어+동사, 의문사 주어+동사, what 주어+동사 등
- He believes that she will be a great writer.   그는 그녀가 위대한 작가가 될 거라고 믿는다.
- We wonder whether he will succeed or not.   우리는 그가 성공할지 못할지 궁금하다.

CF   간접목적어

주어 + 주어의 동사 + 간접목적어 + 직접목적어

'주어는 ~에게 ~을 ~하다'형의 문장에서 '~에게'에 해당하는 말을 '간접목적어'라고 한다. 보통 4형식 문장이라고 한다. 이 때 '~을'에 해당하는 말을 '직접목적어'라고 한다.
- Dad gave me a good present.   아빠는 나에게 좋은 선물을 주었다.
  이 문장에서 me가 간접 목적어, a good present가 직접목적어이다.
- The teacher asked him several questions.   그 선생님은 그에게 여러 질문을 했다.
  이 문장에서 him은 간접목적어, several questions은 직접목적어이다.

4. 보(충)어

보(충)어는 보충해 주는 말이다. 보충어는 명사와 그 친구들, 그리고 형용사와 그 친구들이 쓰일 수 있다.
또 보충어에는 주어를 보충 설명하는 주어 보충어와 목적어를 보충 설명하는 목적어 보충어가 있다.

(1). 주어 보충어
– 주어를 보충 설명하는 말이다. 명사와 형용사가 쓰일 수 있다.

① 명사
- He is a Korean.　　　　　　　　　　　그는 한국인이다.
- Advertisements are arts.　　　　　　　광고는 예술이다.

② 명사의 친구들(to+동사원형, 동사원형ing, 명사절)
- My wish is to meet my son.　　　　　　나의 소망은 나의 아들을 만나는 것이다.
- My hobby is playing baseball.　　　　나의 취미는 야구를 하는 것이다.
- The point is that he is very smart and wise.　핵심은 그가 매우 스마트하고 현명하다는 것이다.

③ 형용사
- The woman is wise.　　　　　　　　　그 여자는 현명하다.

④ 형용사의 친구들 (to+동사원형, 동사원형ing, p.p-과거분사)
- Tina is cooking pork.　　　　　　　　티나는 돼지고기를 요리 중이다.
- Carol is to pass the exam.　　　　　카롤은 그 시험에 합격할 수 있다.
- Her car was broken.　　　　　　　　그녀의 차가 고장 났다.

(2). 목적어 보충어
– 목적어를 보충 설명하는 말이다. 목적어 보충어에도 명사와 형용사 등이 쓰일 수 있다.

① 명사
- They named their daughter Grace.　　그들은 그들의 딸을 그레이스라고 이름 지었다.
- My parents call me Gongju.　　　　　나의 부모는 나를 공주라고 부른다.

② 형용사
- Jason got me angry.　　　　　　　　제이슨은 내가 화나게 했다.
- Students made their rooms neat.　　학생들은 그들의 방을 깨끗하게 만들었다.
- We found the news wrong.　　　　　우리는 그 뉴스가 잘못이라는 것을 알았다.
- His joke makes his classmates merry.　그의 농담은 그의 학급학생들을 즐겁게 한다.

부가 요소들

수 식 어 구

(명사 앞뒤에 쓰인)　　　모든 부사　　　조동사　　　동격
　　형용사

주어, 주어의 동사, 목적어, 보충어(주어보충어, 목적어보충어) 등을 제외한 것들은 문장에서 필수요소가 아닌 것들이다. 부가적인 것들로 명사 앞뒤에서 명사를 꾸며주는 형용사와 동사, 형용사, 다른 부사, 문장전체를 꾸며주는 부사가 대표적이다. 이들을 보통 장식품이라는 뜻의 '수식어구'라고 한다.

1. 명사 앞뒤에 쓰인 형용사

(1) 형용사
- The man entered the dirty room. 그 남자는 더러운 방에 들어갔다.

(2) 형용사의 친구들

① 전치사+명사
- The book on the desk is hers. 책상 위에 있는 책은 그녀의 것이다.

② to 동사원형
- The children have a book to read. 그 아이들은 읽을 책을 가지고 있다.

③ 동사원형ing
- Those swimming boys are happy. 저 수영하고 있는 소년들은 행복하다.

④ p.p-과거분사
- The robber opened the closed door. 그 강도는 닫힌 문을 열었다.

⑤형용사절
- Do you know the man who is running on the track? 너는 그 트랙에서 달리고 있는 중인 남자를 아니?

2. 동사, 형용사, 다른 부사, 문장전체를 꾸며 주는 부사

(1) 부사

① 동사 수식

- Birds <u>fly</u> fast. 새들은 빠르게 난다.

② 형용사 수식

- His muscle is so <u>strong</u>. 그의 근육은 매우 강하다.

③ 다른 부사 수식

- Fish swim very <u>fast</u>. 물고기들이 매우 빠르게 수영한다.

④ 문장전체 수식

- Happily <u>the sailer was saved at the sea</u>. 다행스럽게도 그 돛단배는 바다에서 구조 되었다.

(2) 부사와 그 친구들

① 전치사+명사

- In fact, <u>she is a liar</u>. 실제로 그녀는 거짓말쟁이다.

② to 동사원형

- To meet her, <u>he went to his hometown</u>. 그녀를 만나기 위하여 그는 그의 고향에 갔다.

③ 동사원형ing

- Having no money, <u>he can't have lunch</u>. 그는 돈을 가지고 있지 않기 때문에 점심을 먹을 수 없다.

④ p.p-과거분사

- Tired, <u>he fell asleep in the office room</u>. 피곤했기 때문에 그는 사무실에서 잠들었다.

⑤ 부사절

- As she passed the exam, <u>she was very happy</u>. 그녀가 시험에 합격했기 때문에 매우 행복했다.

3. 기타 부가적인 것들:

이들 이외에 동사를 도와주는 조동사와 명사를 구체적으로 다시 말해주는 동격도 필수적인 것이 아닌 일종의 부가적인 것들이다.

(1) 조동사

- You may join our club.　　　　　　　　　너는 우리의 클럽에 가입해도 돼.
- The students must do their homework.　　학생들은 그들의 숙제를 해야만 한다.

(2) 동격

- You, my friend, are certainly right.(You=my friend)　　내 친구, 너는 확실히 옳아.

memo.

Chapter 01

Nouns & Verbs
명사와 동사

영어에서 핵심품사의 개념은 문장에서 위치를 말한다. 즉 명사(대명사포함)는 문장에서 주어와 목적어, 보충어자리에서 쓰일 수 있다. 한편 동사는 주어 뒤에서 '주어의 동사'만으로 사용 될 수 있다.

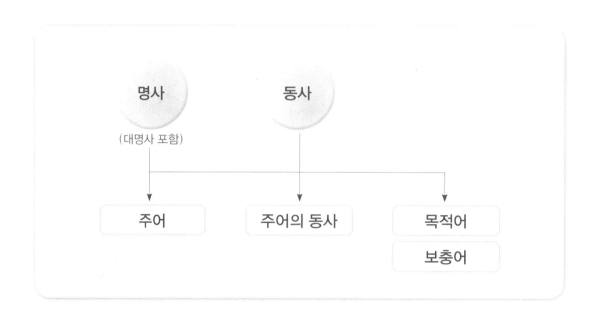

Study 01 명사

명사는 주어, 목적어, 보충어, 동격, 전치사 뒤에 사용된다.

※ 명사란 사람, 동식물, 사물, 개념 등 모든 이름을 말한다.

　ex) William, a lion, a rose, a desk, dream, honesty, etc.

---

① 주어

- <u>Soccer</u> is boring.   축구는 지루해.
- <u>The bird</u> was sad.   새는 슬펐습니다.
- <u>Your throat</u> is a little red.   너의 목이 약간 빨갛다.

② 목적어

- The bird hurt her <u>wings</u>.   그새는 날개를 다쳤습니다.
- Mason made a <u>cage</u> for his bird.   Mason은 그의 새를 위해 새장을 만들었습니다.
- Ten schools founded <u>the Football Association of England</u>.
  10개의 학교는 the Football Association of England를 설립하였다.
- My opponent said <u>bad words</u> to me.   나의 상대편이 내게 심한 말을 했다.
- Some students posted <u>a lot of unkind comments</u>.   몇몇 학생들이 많은 악성 댓글을 달았어요.

③ 보충어

　a). 주어보충어

- This movie will be <u>a big hit</u>.   이 영화는 대히트할거야.
- March is <u>the month</u> when school starts.   3월은 학교가 시작하는 달이다.

　b). 목적어 보충어

- The people elected the candidate <u>president</u>.   국민들은 그 후보를 대통령으로 선출했다.
- My daughter chose the book <u>my birthday present</u>.   나의 딸은 그 책을 나의 생일선물로 골라 주었다.

다만 보충어자리에 형용사도 쓰인다.

　[주어 보충어]

- The problem was so <u>difficult</u>.   그 문제는 너무나 어려웠다.
- My photo was <u>clear</u> there.   내 사진은 거기에 선명했다.

[목적어 보충어]

- We found the babies <u>sad</u>.　　　　　　우리는 아이들이 슬프다는 것을 발견했다.
- The students make the teacher **happy**.　학생들은 선생님을 행복하게 한다.

④ 전치사 뒤

- The baby bird fell <u>out of</u> **a tree**.　　　그 아기 새는 나무에서 떨어졌다.
- Disease should be treated <u>at</u> **the beginning**.　병은 초기에 치료받아야 한다.
- Soccer was a regular subject <u>in</u> **many public schools** <u>in</u> **England** <u>in</u> **the early 1800s**.

　　　　　　　　　　　　　　　축구는 1800년대 영국의 공립학교에서 정규과목이었다.

 확인문제 1

다음 문장에서 명사(대명사포함)를 모두 찾으시오.

(01). The crowd cheered.

(02). People drive too fast.

(03). My throat really hurts.

(04). Schools start in that month.

(05). My children make noises.

(06). I have a terrible headache.

(07). Mason found a baby bird.

(08). We call the shepherd a liar.

(09). We couldn't solve the problem.

(10). The rock was too heavy for us to lift.

〈정답과 해설 019〉

Study 02 동사

동사는 보통 주어 뒤에 '주어의 동사'로 쓰인다.

* 동사란 동작이나 상태를 나타내는 말이다.

동작– go, move, fight, etc.

상태– want, know, have, etc.

- That <u>sounds</u> good.
- My mom <u>expects</u> me to be a doctor.
- They really <u>care</u> about you.
- My mom <u>lets</u> me play games.

좋은 생각이구나.

우리 엄마는 내가 의사가 되기를 기대하신다.

그들은 정말 여러분에게 관심을 쏟으신다.

나의 엄마는 내가 게임을 하도록 허락하신다.

CF 동사 앞에 조동사가 올 수 있다.

You <u>can</u> make more friends there.

넌 거기서 더 많은 친구들을 사귈 수 있을 거야.

The boys <u>will</u> have a basketball game.

남학생들은 축구 시합을 할 것이다.

Young people <u>can</u> experience winter sports through the program.

청소년들은 이 프로그램을 통해 겨울 스포츠를 경험할 수 있다.

CF 'There + 동사+ 주어 ~' 에서는 주어가 동사 뒤에 온다.

There is <u>a castle</u> in the forest.

숲속에 성이 있다.

There are <u>many ants</u> in the ground.

땅바닥에 많은 개미가 있다.

다음 각 문장에서 동사를 찾으시오.

(01). We also talk a lot.

(02). I practice the guitar.

(03). We know your parents well.

(04). The players calm down.

(05). The Africans learned to ski.

(06). They became good friends.

(07). The kids may join the club.

(08). What happened to Willy's eye?

(09). Little Willy loved this country.

(10). We cheer for our national team.

Study 03   동사와 명사

1. 동사와 명사의 형태가 같은 것

한 단어가 명사와 동사, 두 가지 모두로 사용되는 단어도 많다. 명사냐 동사냐는 오직 **사용되는 위치**에 따라 달라진다.
주어, 목적어, 보충어, 전치사 뒤에서 사용되면 명사이고 주어의 동사(보통 주어 뒤)로 쓰였으면 동사이다.

a). pay 동사: 지불하다/ 명사: 급료

- 동사 I <u>pay</u> the house rent monthly.   나는 집세를 월세로 지불한다.
- 명사 The company raised the worker's <u>pay</u>.   그 회사는 노동자의 임금을 올렸다.

b). fly 동사: 날다/ 명사: 파리

- 동사 Birds <u>fly</u> over the tree.   새들이 나무 위에서 난다.
- 명사 The <u>flies</u> gather in the garbage can.   파리들이 쓰레기통에 모인다.

c). bond 동사: 유대를 맺다/ 명사: 결속

- 동사 The workers <u>bond</u> strongly each other.   노동자들은 서로 강하게 연대한다.
- 명사 She and I have a special <u>bond</u>.   그녀와 나는 특별한 유대감을 가지고 있다.

d). bar 동사: 막다, 금하다/ 명사: 막대기, 장애물

- 동사 The police <u>barred</u> the parade of the citizens.   경찰은 시민들의 행진을 방해했다.
- 명사 There were <u>bars</u> across the windows of the prison.

감옥의 창문을 가로질러 (탈출)예방 장애물이 있었다.

 확인문제 3

다음 아래 쌍으로 이루어진 문장들에서 밑줄 친 단어가 명사로 사용된 것인지 동사를 사용된 것인지를 말하시오. 그리고 해석하시오.

(01). score   동사: 득점하다/ 명사: 점수

  ⓐ The player <u>scored</u> better in the game. (　　　　　　　)

  ⓑ The student's <u>score</u> got worse. (　　　　　　)

(02). water   동사: 물주다/ 명사: 물

  ⓐ The <u>water</u> of this well is very good for health. (　　　　　　)

  ⓑ Dad <u>watered</u> the flowers in the garden. (　　　　　　)

(03). twist   동사: 비틀다/ 명사: 비틀기

  ⓐ The dancer <u>twisted</u> his body. (　　　　　)

  ⓑ The dancer did the <u>twist</u> before the performance. (　　　　　)

(04). capture   동사: 붙잡다/ 명사: 포획, 저장

  ⓐ The soldiers <u>captured</u> the runway soldier. (　　　　　)

  ⓑ He was released yesterday after the <u>capture</u> by the terrorist. (　　　　　)

(05). broadcast   동사: 방송하다/ 명사: 방송

  ⓐ I watch a live <u>broadcast</u> of the football game. (　　　　　)

  ⓑ BBC <u>broadcasts</u> to all parts of the world. (　　　　　)

(06). change   동사: 바꾸다/ 명사: 교환

  ⓐ The <u>change</u> of habit is difficult. (　　　　　)

  ⓑ The boy and the girl <u>changed</u> their seats. (　　　　　)

(07). progress   동사: 발전하다/ 명사: 진보

  ⓐ History <u>progresses</u>. (　　　　　)

  ⓑ The <u>progress</u> of history is with us. (　　　　　)

(08). preview   동사: 미리보다/ 명사: 시사회, 서문

  ⓐ This book gives us a <u>preview</u> of life in the 25th century. (　　　　　)

  ⓑ The audience <u>previewed</u> the film with characters. (　　　　　)

(09). overthrow   동사: 전복시키다/ 명사: 전복

  ⓐ The people <u>overthrew</u> the dictatorship. (　　　　　)

  ⓑ The soldiers are prepared for the sudden <u>overthrow</u>. (　　　　　)

(10). transfer   동사: 전학하다, 이동시키다, 갈아타다/ 명사: 전근

     ⓐ You can <u>transfer</u> to number two line. (   )

     ⓑ She is hoping for a <u>transfer</u> to another part of the company. (   )

《정답과 해설 21》

2. 동사와 명사의 형태가 다른 것

형태(formation)	예(examples)
동사+tion	predict → prediction 예언 produce → production 생산 apply → application 적용 receive → reception 수락
동사+sion	conclude → conclusion 결론 decide → decision 결정 discuss → discussion 토론
동사+ment	move → movement 움직임 develop → development 발전
동사+al	arrive → arrival 도착 deny → denial 부인 approve → approval 승인 survive → survival 생존
동사+ry	deliver → delivery 배달 discover → discovery 발견
기타 (+ence/-ance/-ure/-ive/-ity)	differ 다르다 → difference 차이 appear 나타나다 → appearance 출연, 외모 fail 실패하다 → failure 실패 relate 관련되다 → relative 친척 represent 대표하다 → representative 직원 vary 다양하다 → variety 다양성 secure 안전하게 하다 → security 안전

a). dismiss 동사: (의견 따위를) 무시하다. 해고하다. / dismissal 명사: 해고, 퇴학

- The company <u>dismissed</u> 100 employees last month.   그 회사는 지난달 100명의 직원들을 해고했다.
- Those workers are protesting against their <u>dismissal</u>.   저 노동자들은 그들의 해고에 대해 항의하고 있는 중이다.

b). expand 동사: 확장하다 / expansion 명사: 확대

- The classes <u>expanded</u> to the 3rd and 4th graders in 2010.

                         2010년에는 3~4학년으로 교육 대상을 확대했다.

- Trees prevent the <u>expansion</u> of yellow dust storms here.

                        나무들이 그 황사폭풍의 확장을 예방한다.

c). infect 동사: 감염시키다 / infection 명사: 감염

• I might **infect** other children.　　　　　　다른 아이들에게 감염시킬 수도 있다.

• My eyes were bloodshot because of the **infection**.　　감염되어서 눈이 충혈 되었어.

d). react 동사: 반응하다 / reaction 명사: 반응

• The special micro sensors under robot skin **react** to human touch.

　　　　　　로봇의 표면 아래 특별한 작은 센서가 인간의 터치에 반응한다.

• The dust or smell from peanuts can trigger a **reaction**.　땅콩의 가루나 냄새가 반응을 일으킬 수 있어.

e). translate 동사: 이식하다 / translation 명사: 이식, 번역

• The computer program **translates** thoughts into electronic images.

　　　　　　그 컴퓨터 프로그램은 생각을 전자 이미지로 바꿉니다.

• The traditional poetry is revived in an English **translation**.

　　　　　　이 전통의 시가 영어로 번역되어 새로이 부활한다.

 확인문제 4

다음 단어들의 명사형을 쓰시오. 또 명사형의 뜻을 쓰시오.

(01). develop → _____, _____

(02). predict → _____, _____

(03). decide → _____, _____

(04). produce → _____, _____

(05). apply → _____, _____

(06). deny → _____, _____

(07). discover → _____, _____

(08). approve → _____, _____

(09). discuss → _____, _____

(10). receive → _____, _____

(11). conclude → _____, _____

(12). move → _____, _____

(13). arrive → _____, _____

(14). deliver → _____, _____

《정답과 해설 2P》

3. -er/-or는 '~하는 사람'등

a). -er형

sing-singer 가수   teach-teacher 선생님   run-runner 달리기 선수
write-writer 작가   farm-farmer 농부   interpret-interpreter 해설가

b). -or형

act-actor 배우   edit-editor 편집자   invent-inventor 발명가
collet-collector 수집가   illustrate-illustrator 삽화가   direct-director 감독
counsel-counselor 상담가   translate-translator 번역가

CF   cook은 동사-요리하다, 명사-요리사의 뜻으로 쓰이며 cooker는 요리기구이다.

 확인문제 5

다음 동사의 '~하는 사람' 명사형을 쓰시오.

(01). write → _____   (02). farm → _____

(03). teach → _____   (04). run → _____

(05). direct → _____   (06). invent → _____

(07). collet → _____   (08). sing → _____

《정답과 해설 2P》

further study

명사처럼 주어, 목적어, 보충어 등에 사용할 수 있는 것들

- 명사
- 대명사
- to 동사원형
- 동사원형ing
- 명사절(that 주어+동사~, whether 주어+동사 ~ 등, 의문사 주어+동사 ~ 등)

1. 명사

- The flight was canceled due to bad weather.
- The passengers want magazines to read.

그 비행기는 나쁜 날씨 때문에 취소되었다.

승객들은 읽을 잡지를 원한다.

2. 대명사

- He offered a suggestion about the matter.
- Please, show me another.

그는 그 문제에 관해 제안을 했다.

제발 나에게 또 다른 것을 보여 주세요.

3. to 동사원형

- To make money is not easy.
- Cinderella wanted to win a gold medal.

돈을 버는 것은 쉽지 않다.

신데렐라는 금메달을 받는 것을 원했다.

4. 동사원형ing

- Smoking is harmful.
- They enjoy climbing mountains.

흡연은 해롭다.

그들은 산을 오르는 것을 즐긴다.

5. 명사절

- Our problem is that we are very tired now.
- One question is whether she is a liar or not.
- Our wonder is why she ran away.

우리의 문제는 지금 우리가 매우 피곤하다는 것이다.
한 가지 의문은 그녀가 거짓말쟁이인가 아닌가이다.
우리의 궁금함은 왜 그녀가 도망 쳤는가이다.

 확인문제 6

다음 문장에서 주어를 찾으시오. 그리고 해석하시오.

(01). We use a balance scale for comparing weight.

(02). A liquid has both weight and volume.

(03). Volume is the amount a container can hold.

(04). Putting trash in landfills keeps it from becoming pollution.

(05). The professor suggested that his family move to the country.

〈정답과 해설 2P〉

 확인문제 7

다음 문장에서 목적어를 찾으시오. 그리고 해석하시오.

(01). People transmit message on the Internet.

(02). They stopped studying in the classroom.

(03). Mom promised to buy me a new cell phone.

(04). The producer said that the story is true.

(05). Humans need to take good care of trees and animals.

〈정답과 해설 2P〉

다음 문장에서 주어 보충어를 찾으시오. 그리고 해석하시오

(01). The goal of every company is to make a profit.

(02). Thomas Edison was one of the world's greatest inventors.

(03). Coal, gas, and oil are energy sources.

(04). Human resources are people and the skills they have.

(05). The duty of the organization is sponsoring fund.

Grammar in Reading

〈정답과 해설 3P〉

1. 다음 글에서 각 문장의 주어를 찾으시오.

ⓐ Pigeons can see a very long distance —about 2,000 feet. ⓑ That's why the Navy train them to look for orange color, the color of life jackets. In bad weather, ⓒ sea waves can break boats and drown people. When that happens, ⓓ there is no time to waste. ⓔ Pigeons help with the rescue. ⓕ They ride in a helicopter with the Navy crew. ⓖ They find the orange life jackets very quickly. ⓗ So the crew can act quickly to save people."

01. ⓐ-   02. ⓑ-   03. ⓒ-   04. ⓓ-
05. ⓔ-   06. ⓕ-   07. ⓖ-   08. ⓗ-

2. 다음 글에서 각각의 문장에서 주어의 동사를 찾으시오.

ⓐ Tom lives next to my house. ⓑ We are friends. ⓒ We go to school together everyday. ⓓ Jane and John live near my house. ⓔ They are our teachers. ⓕ Jane is our English teacher, and ⓖ John is our art teacher. ⓗ They go to school together, too. ⓘ I think that ⓙ Jane and John are just friends, but ⓚ Tom thinks that ⓛ they are brother and sister. ⓜ I want to ask them, "ⓝ I think that you are just friends, but ⓞ Tom thinks that you are brother and sister. ⓟ Who is right?"

01. ⓐ-   02. ⓑ-   03. ⓒ-   04. ⓓ-
05. ⓔ-   06. ⓕ-   07. ⓖ-   08. ⓗ-
09. ⓘ-   10. ⓙ-   11. ⓚ-   12. ⓛ-
13. ⓜ-   14. ⓝ-   15. ⓞ-   16. ⓟ-

Grammar in Reading

《정답과 해설 31》

3. 다음 글의 밑줄 친 부분이 각 문장에서 주어보충어인지 목적어인지를 구별하시오.

I know ⓐ <u>five people</u>. The first woman is ⓑ <u>Jane</u>. She is a dancer. The second woman is ⓒ <u>Maria</u>. She is my sister. She is a nurse. She helps ⓓ <u>many patients</u>. The third man is ⓔ <u>my father</u>. He is a taxi driver. He drives ⓕ <u>his taxi</u> everyday. The fifth man is my brother. He is a pianist. He plays ⓖ <u>the piano</u> very well. Who is the fourth man? It is me. I am a painter.

01. ⓐ-　　　　02. ⓑ-　　　　03. ⓒ-　　　　04. ⓓ-
05. ⓔ-　　　　06. ⓕ-　　　　07. ⓖ-

4. 다음 글의 밑줄 친 문장에서 목적어를 찾으시오.,

ⓐ. <u>I have a baby cat</u>. It is a kitten. ⓑ. <u>It likes to play and drink lots of milk</u>. ⓒ. <u>Tom has a baby dog</u>. It is a puppy. ⓓ. <u>It likes to chew an old shoe</u>. It runs and barks. My grandfather is a farmer. ⓔ. <u>He has many animals</u>. ⓕ. <u>He has a baby sheep</u>. It is a lamb. It eats grass. He has a baby duck. It is a duckling. It swims with its wide feet. ⓖ. <u>I can see an eagle in my grandfather's farm</u>. It flies high and fast. My grandfather lives in an old house. ⓗ. <u>He likes his old house</u>.

01. ⓐ-　　　　02. ⓑ-　　　　03. ⓒ-　　　　04. ⓓ-
05. ⓔ-　　　　06. ⓕ-　　　　07. ⓖ-　　　　08. ⓗ-

《정답과 해설 11》

1. 다음 각 동사에 해당하는 '～하는 사람'에 해당하는 단어를 쓰시오.

01. believe –

02. illustrate –

03. counsel –

04. translate –

05. interpret –

06. act –

07. edit –

08. cook –

09. support –

10. interview –

2. 아래 각각의 문장에서 동사에 밑줄을 긋고 해석하시오.

01. We need more than 8 players.
( )

02. We need something to ride on.
( )

03. You celebrate your parents' birthdays every year.
( )

04. The girls can play badminton.
( )

05. Our team lost the basketball game.
(   )

06. Our players practiced very hard.
(   )

07. Students should not use cell phones at school.
(   )

08. My best friend moved to a new city.
(   )

09. I practiced again and again with your help.
(   )

10. We have a multi-sports event next month.
(   )

11. Unfortunately, we missed the last shot.
(   )

12. Many people wrote nice comments to cheer me up anonymously.
(   )

3. 다음 문장에서 각각 동사와 명사(대명사포함)를 모두 말하시오.

01. August in Korea is the hot day.
동사: _____   명사:_____

02. The boys can swim across the river.
동사: _____   명사:_____

03. I'll never forget the experiences there.
동사: _____   명사:_____

《정답과 해설 11》

04. We must respect the rights of others.

동사: _____ 명사: _____

05. The divers will save the drowning boys.

동사: _____ 명사: _____

06. Pele scored the most goals at that time.

동사: _____ 명사: _____

07. January in South Korea is the cold month.

동사: _____ 명사: _____

08. Bill Gates is one of the richest men in the world.

동사: _____ 명사: _____

09. The players visited Pyeongchang with my family.

동사: _____ 명사: _____

10. The man checked the library's Lost and Found?

동사: _____ 명사: _____

11. They learned one of the Winter Olympic Games.

동사: _____ 명사: _____

12. Searchlight pulled the sled down Main Street past the crowd.

동사: _____ 명사: _____

4. 다음 아래 쌍으로 이루어진 문장들에서 밑줄 친 단어가 명사로 사용된 것인지 동사로 사용된 것인지를 말하시오. 그리고 해석하시오.

01. approach 동사: 접근하다/ 명사: 접근

ⓐ His approach to the woman is unusual.

(,   )

ⓑ The believers in Christianity approached the pope.

(,   )

02. duplicate 동사: (서류를) 복사하다/ 명사: 복사본

    ⓐ I have the duplicate of the contract paper.
        (,   )
    ⓑ The instructor duplicated the column in the newspaper.
        (,   )

03. charge 동사: 비난하다. 요금을 청구하다. 고발하다/ 명사: 요금, 책임

    ⓐ President is in charge of the tragedy.
        (,   )
    ⓑ The people charged president due to the fraud election.
        (,   )

04. discharge 동사: 해임시키다, 방출하다/ 명사: 해임, 퇴원, 석방

    ⓐ Discharge is not right.
        (,   )
    ⓑ President discharged the minister because of the accident.
        (,   )

05. cast 동사: 배우를 정하다/ 명사: 출연배우들

    ⓐ The movie director cast me as a leading actor.
        (,   )
    ⓑ The movie has a strong cast that includes several famous actresses.
        (,   )

06. contrast 동사: 대조하다/ 명사: 대조

    ⓐ These artists use contrast.
        (,   )
    ⓑ In her speech she contrasted her aim with his achievement.
        (,   )

《정답과 해설 51》

07. support 동사: 지지하다/ 명사: 지지

  ⓐ The people strongly support democracy.
    (　　　　　　,　　　　　　　　　　　　)
  ⓑ The support for democracy doesn't end.
    (　　　　　　,　　　　　　　　　　　　)

08. advance 동사: 전진하다/ 명사: 전진

  ⓐ Democracy advances.
    (　　　　　　,　　　　　　　　　　　　)
  ⓑ The advance of democracy is essential.
    (　　　　　　,　　　　　　　　　　　　)

09. autograph 동사: 자필서명하다/ 명사: 자필서명

  ⓐ This autograph is not effective.
    (　　　　　　,　　　　　　　　　　　　)
  ⓑ They autograph on the contract paper.
    (　　　　　　,　　　　　　　　　　　　)

10. account 동사: ~의 원인의 설명해 주다/ 명사: 계좌, 설명

  ⓐ How do you account for losing five games in a row?
    (　　　　　　,　　　　　　　　　　　　)
  ⓑ Please give us your account of what happened.
    (　　　　　　,　　　　　　　　　　　　)

11. transplant 동사: 이식하다/ 명사: 이식

  ⓐ This surgeon has done several kidney transplants.
    (　　　　　　,　　　　　　　　　　　　)
  ⓑ The doctor transplanted the liver of the donator to the patient.
    (　　　　　　,　　　　　　　　　　　　)

12. debate 동사: 논쟁하다/ 명사: 토론

ⓐ There is no end to this debate.
(,   )

ⓑ They debate about the effectiveness of education.
(,   )

13. exchange 동사: 교환하다/ 명사: 교환

ⓐ The two teams exchanged presents before the game.
(,   )

ⓑ There was an exchange of political prisoners between the two countries.
(,   )

14. exhaust 동: 지치게 하다, 모두 사용하다./ 명: 배기가스

ⓐ The city is filled with exhaust.
(,   )

ⓑ We have exhausted our supply of oxygen.
(,   )

15. display 동사: 진열하다/ 명사: 전시, 진열

ⓐ The goods were on display in the shop window.
(,   )

ⓑ The merchant displayed fruits in the shop window.
(,   )

5. 다음 각 쌍으로 되어 있는 문장에서 밑줄 친 문장이 동사인지 명사인지를 말하시오. 그리고 각각 해석하시오.

01. ⓐ I explained the situation to her.
(,   )

ⓑ Images were much better than a long-written explanation.
(,   )

중간 · 기말고사 내신만점대비문제

《정답과 해설 51P》

02. ⓐ Our predictions are usually correct.

   (,   )

   ⓑ No one can predict the result of a soccer match.

   (,   )

03. ⓐ Icicle removal has become a new scene.

   (,   )

   ⓑ The students removed dust from your clothes and skin.

   (,   )

04. ⓐ Recycling is also important for our future.

   (,   )

   ⓑ We must recycle used bottles.

   (,   )

05. ⓐ Could you tell me the flight number and the time of departure?

   (,   )

   ⓑ The express train to Bristol departs from platform 21.

   (,   )

06. ⓐ Do you know how many tastes your tongue can detect?

   (,   )

   ⓑ The detective decided to have the suspects watched 24 hours a day.

   (,   )

07. ⓐ Boring will declare itself Dull's sister community on May 5.

   (,   )

   ⓑ On July 4, 1776, we adopted the Declaration of Independence.

   (,   )

08. ⓐ Exposure to radiation can damage biological cells and cause cancer.

   (,   )

   ⓑ The public exposed their selective data.

   (,   )

09.ⓐ Currently, customers can only withdraw about $383 in cash daily.
(,   )

ⓑ They had demanded the withdrawal of Korean troops from Iraq.
(,   )

10.ⓐ Did Joe get a letter of acceptance from the university?
(,   )

ⓑ Although the school accepts very few children, it is free.
(,   )

6. 다음 짝으로 이루어진 문장에 주어진 동사와 명사 중 하나를 넣어서 문장을 완성하시오. 동사의 경우, 필요한 경우 문장 끝의 시제 등에 유념하여 적절한 형태를 적절하게 쓰시오. 그리고 각각 해석하시오.

01. differ 동사: 다르다/ difference 명사: 차이(점)

ⓐ My interpretation of this artwork (   ) from hers. (현재시제)
(,   )

ⓑ We can reduce our opinion (   ) through talk.
(,   )

02. depress 동사: 우울하게 하다/ depression 명사: 우울

ⓐ Bad economy (   ) the people. (현재시제)
(,   )

ⓑ A lack of sleep is result into (   ).
(,   )

03. suggest 동사: 제안하다/ suggestion 명사: 제안

ⓐ Here are some (   ).
(,   )

ⓑ Achor (   ) that you see the positive things in your life. (현재시제)
(,   )

(정답과 해설 6P)

04. select 동사: 선택하다/ selection 명사: 선택

Ⓜ (   ) of the attack unit is still in progress.
(,   )

Ⓡ You may (   ) the book you want to read.
(,   )

05. consider 동사: 고려하다/ consideration 명사: 고려

Ⓜ We (   ) the place and time. (현재)
(,   )

Ⓡ (   ) of cost is important.
(,   )

06. donate 기증하다/ donation 명사: 기증

Ⓜ People must (   ) to the poor.
(,   )

Ⓡ The more (   ) is needed to the poor.
(,   )

07. protect 동사: 보호하다/ protection 명사: 보호

Ⓜ We must (   ) the Earth before it's too late!
(,   )

Ⓡ Children campaign nature (   ) in the street.
(,   )

08. invest 동사: 투자하다/ investment 명사: 투자

Ⓜ One must (   ) his or her time and finances.
(,   )

Ⓡ There is a lack of (   ) in security.
(,   )

09. revive 동사: 되살아나다/ revival 명사: 부활

    ⓐ Two Koreas should (   ) the long-stalled talks.
    (,   )
    ⓑ Spring represents (   ).
    (,   )

10. recover 동사: 되살아나다/ recovery 명사: 회복

    ⓐ Patients (   ) from new treatment. (과거)
    (,   )
    ⓑ Since then the economy has been on a very fast (   ).
    (,   )

7. 다음 문장에서 각각 주어를 찾으시오.

01. The cat is on my desk.

02. The moon rises at 7:30 p.m.

03. They are walking in the park.

04. My cousin Susan will arrive soon.

05. The pharmacy is across from the hospital.

06. The woman heard Harry go out.

07. My mother exercises in the park on Sundays.

08. Ms. William's children are always arguing.

09. The plants are growing nicely in the greenhouse.

10. The criminal didn't allow me to leave the room.

8. 다음 문장에서 각각 목적어를 찾으시오.

01. The children found the puzzle difficult.

02. He painted his room a shade of blue.

03. She will tell the secret to you.

04. I brought some blankets to them.

05. The boy wrote a fan letter to Rain.

06. The baseball player hit the ball over the fence.

07. She will get the concert tickets for me.

08. Julia sometimes buys robots for her son.

09. The teacher asked a few questions of him.

10. He will build a beautiful tree house for her.

11. My father cooked a delicious meal for me.

12. The university has awarded $500 scholarship to her.

9. 다음 문장에서 각각 주어 보충어(01-05)와 목적어 보충어(06-10)를 찾으시오.

(주어보충어)
01. The play was very good.

02. Your feet smell terrible.

03. She is a professor in the college.

04. The man was a boss of the company.

05. She became the CEO of the company in 2006.

(목적어 보충어)
06. He called me a fool yesterday in class.

07. The movie got her a big star.

08. The adults made the worker their slave.

09. His parents made him a leader of the country.

10. Our classmates elected him the chairman of our class.

10. 다음 문장에서 전치사 뒤의 명사를 찾으시오.

01. My daughter was at the library.

02. The cat is on my desk.

03. The moon rises at 7:30 p.m.

04. They are walking in the park.

05. My friends saw Jeremy sleep at his desk earlier.

06. The pharmacy is across from the hospital.

07. The plants are growing nicely in the greenhouse.

08. The girls gained weight on vacation.

Chapter

02

Adjective & Adverb
형용사와 부사

Study 01   형용사와 부사의 쓰임

형용사는 명사의 졸병이다. 부사는 원래 동사의 졸병으로 태어났으나 형용사나, 다른 부사, 문장전체의 졸병역할 까지 한다.

1. 형용사

형용사는 명사의 졸병으로 명사 앞이나 뒤, 주어보충어, 목적어보충어자리에서 사용된다.
명사 앞에서 뒤에 오는 명사, 명사 뒤에서 앞에 오는 명사를 꾸며준다. 또 주어 보충어자리에서 주어(명사)를, 목적어 보충어자리에서 목적어(명사)를 꾸며준다.

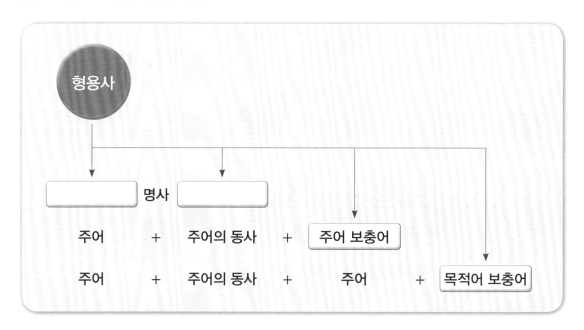

① 명사 앞

- The <u>peaceful</u> **village** is full of visitors.   그 평화로운 마을은 방문객들로 가득 찼다.
- The <u>friendly</u> **animals** came up to the girl.   그 친근한 동물들은 소녀에게로 다가왔다.

② 명사 뒤

- The village <u>peaceful</u> to the visitors is famous for historical sites.

  방문객들에게 평화스러운 마을은 역사적인 장소들로 유명하다.

- The people <u>friendly</u> to the animals protested against the cruelty to animals.

  그 동물들에게 우호적인 사람들은 동물에게 잔인함에 대항하여 저항했다.

③ 주어 보충어

- The village is <u>peaceful</u> to the visitors.　　　그 마을은 방문객들에게 평화롭다.
- The people are <u>friendly</u> to the animals.　　　그 사람들은 동물들에게 우호적이다.

④ 목적어 보충어

- The village people made **their village** <u>peaceful</u>.　　　그 마을 사람들은 그들의 마을을 평화롭게 만들었다.
- The campaign made **the people** <u>friendly</u> to the animals.

  그 캠페인은 사람들이 동물들에게 우호적으로 만들었다.

🔍 확인문제 1

밑줄 그은 형용사가 꾸며주는 명사를 말하시오.

(형용사는 명사앞이나 뒤, 주어보충어, 목적어 보충어자리에서 사용된다.)

(01). The man is <u>handsome</u>.

(02). We made the hole <u>bigger</u>.

(03). Her song makes us <u>energetic</u>.

(04). That is a most <u>wonderful</u> idea.

(05). The room <u>full</u> of books is clean.

(06). The <u>beautiful</u> woman is my girlfriend.

(07). Do you know the man <u>angry</u> at the lady?

(08). I happened to see something <u>strange</u> there.

〈정답과 해설 7P〉

2. 부사

부사는 동사, 형용사, 다른 부사, 문장전체의 졸병으로 동사 앞뒤, 형용사나 부사 앞, 문장 맨 앞이나 뒤에서 사용된다.

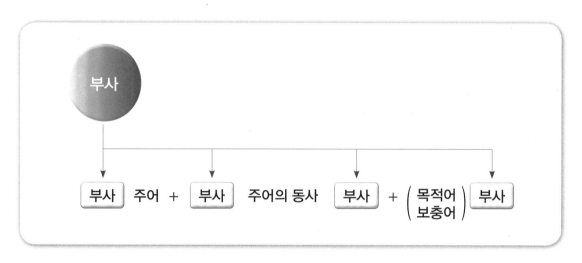

① 동사 뒤

- Something **happens** <u>suddenly</u>. 무엇인가 갑자기 발생한다.
- The soldiers **danced** <u>peacefully</u> on the stage. 군인들은 무대에서 평화롭게 춤췄다.

② 동사 앞

- The soldiers <u>peacefully</u> **danced** on the stage. 군인들은 평화롭게 무대에서 춤추었다.
- The bus <u>always</u> **arrives** at the corner of my street at 4:00.

  버스는 항상 나의 거리의 코너에 4시에 도착한다.

- The marathoner <u>finally</u> **crossed** the finish line after five hours of running.

  그 마라토너는 다섯 시간을 달린 후 마침내 결승전을 통과했다.

③ 형용사 앞

- The man is <u>really</u> **handsome**.　　　　　　　　　　　그 남자는 정말 잘생겼다.

④ 다른 부사 앞

- The couple can dance <u>quite</u> **well**.　　　　　　　　　그 부부는 꽤 잘 춤 줄 수 있다.

④ 문장 맨 앞이나 맨 뒤

- <u>Peacefully</u> the soldiers danced on the stage.　　　평화롭게 그 군인들은 무대에서 춤췄다.
- The dancers danced on the stage <u>merrily</u>.　　　　그 댄서들은 무대에서 즐겁게 춤추었다.

🔍 확인문제 2

다음 문장에서 밑줄 그은 부사가 꾸며주는 말을 말하시오.
(부사는 동사, 형용사, 부사, 문장전체를 꾸며준다.)

(01). Everything moved so <u>fast</u>.

(02). The girl grew up so <u>quickly</u>.

(03). My wife and girls are <u>already</u> asleep.

(04). He <u>really</u> enjoyed the manual work.

(05). He <u>practically</u> lives in the office.

(06). Alice is a <u>very</u> smart person.

(07). <u>Absolutely</u>, Alice is a perfect student.

(08). <u>Maybe</u> she will come back soon.

(09). Jared's shoelaces was tied <u>together</u>.

(10). The room is warm <u>enough</u> to sleep well.

(11). He realized <u>too</u> late that he had left his bag in the bus.

(12). You <u>just</u> make me a cup of green tea on Monday evening.

〈정답과 해설 7P〉

Study 02 형용사와 부사의 형태

–ly형의 단어는 형용사와 부사가 있다. '명사+ly'는 형용사이고 '형용사+ly'는 부사이다. 부사가 압도적으로 많다.

형용사	부사
명사 + ly	형용사 + ly

1. 형용사 (명사+ly)

- wool+ly → woolly   모직의
- love+ly → lovely   사랑스러운
- quarter+ly → quarterly   분기의
- time+ly → timely   적시의
- day+ly → daily   매일의
- week+ly → weekly   매주의
- month+ly → monthly   매달의
- year+ly → yearly   매년의
- order+ly → orderly   질서정연한
- friend+ly → friendly   우호적인
- coward+ly → cowardly   비겁한
- man+ly → manly   남자다운
- ghost+ly → ghostly   유령 같은
- beast +ly → beastly   야수 같은
- body +ly → bodily   신체의

다만 daily, weekly, monthly, quarterly, yearly 등은 부분적으로 부사로도 쓰인다.
- The shepherd went to the forest <u>daily</u>.   그 목동은 매일 숲으로 갔다.
- The princess called the woodman <u>weekly</u>.   그 공주는 나무꾼에게 매주 전화했다.

명사+y → 형용사

다만 다음단어는 명사에 y만을 붙여서 형용사를 만든다.

hair+y → hairy	털투성이의
luck+y → lucky	행운의
cloud+y → cloudy	흐린
rain+y → rainy	비 오는
snow+y → snowy	눈 오는

다만 '단모음+단자음'으로 끝나는 경우, 마지막 자음을 한 번 더 쓰고 y를 붙여야 한다.

fur+y → furry	모피의
sun+y → sunny	맑은
fog+y → foggy	안개 낀

기타– '–ly'형태 형용사

lonely	외로운

 ## 확인문제 3

다음 단어들의 형용사형을 쓰시오. 또 형용사형의 뜻을 쓰시오.

(01). wool → _____, _____

(02). love → _____, _____

(03). quarter → _____, _____

(04). time → _____, _____

(05). day → _____, _____

(06). week → _____, _____

(07). month → _____, _____

(08). year → _____, _____

(09). order → _____, _____

(10). friend → _____, _____

<정답과 해설 7P>

2. 부사(형용사+ly)

일반적인 경우	특별한 경우	
형용사+ly	자음+y로 끝나는 경우	자음+ily
	easy→ easily, lucky→ luckily, heavy → heavily, angry→ angrily	
fair → fairly soft → softly wise → wisely private→ privately sudden→ suddenly	-le로 끝나는 경우	-le→-ly
	terrible→ terribly, gentle→ gently, simple →simply	
	-ue로 끝나는 경우	-ue→-uly
	true →truly	
	-ll로 끝나는 경우	-y만 붙인다
	full → fully, dull →dully	

① 형용사+ly형 부사

- nice+ly → nicely   멋지게
- clean+ly → cleanly   깨끗하게
- total+ly → totally   전체적으로
- remote+ly → remotely   멀리
- extreme+ly → extremely   극단적으로
- recent+ly → recently   최근에
- equal+ly → equally   똑같이
- dependent +ly → dependently   의존적으로
- universal+ly → universally   보편적으로
- delicious+ly → deliciously   맛있게
- fortunate+ly → fortunately   다행스럽게
- effective +ly → effectively   효과적으로
- important+ly → importantly   중요하게

② 자음+y는 y를 i로 고치고 +ly

- happy +ly → happily   행복하게
- gloomy+ly → gloomily   우울하게
- merry+ly → merrily   즐겁게
- necessary +ly → necessarily   필수적으로
- ordinary +ly → ordinarily   일반적으로

③ -le로 끝나는 경우 -le를 -ly로
- simple →simply   단순하게
- gentle→ gently   부드럽게
- terrible→ terribly   끔찍하게

④ -ic로 끝나는 경우 -ally
- dramatic+ally → dramatically   극적으로
- economic+ally → economically   경제적으로

 확인문제 4

다음 단어들의 뜻을 쓰고 형용사의 부사형을 만드시오.

(01). happy   →   _____ , _____

(02). kind   →   _____ , _____

(03). noisy   →   _____ , _____

(04). wise   →   _____ , _____

(05). fair   →   _____ , _____

(06). pure   →   _____ , _____

(07). clear   →   _____ , _____

(08). regular   →   _____ , _____

(09). usual   →   _____ , _____

(10). actual   →   _____ , _____

(11). precise   →   _____ , _____

(12). real   →   _____ , _____

(13). legal   →   _____ , _____

(14). lawful   →   _____ , _____

(15). neat → _____, _____

(16). tidy → _____, _____

(17). especial → _____, _____

(18). special → _____, _____

(19). definite → _____, _____

(20). recent → _____, _____

Level UP

형용사와 부사가 동일한 경우:

A. 한단어가 형용사와 부사 두 가지로 쓰인다.

	형용사	부사
fast	빠른	빠르게
long	긴	길게
enough	충분한	충분히
early	이른	일찍
daily	매일의, 일간의	매일
weekly	매주의, 주간의	매주
monthly	매월의, 월간의	매월
quarterly	분기의	분기마다
yearly	매년의, 연간의	매년

① 형용사

Don't eat a <u>fast</u> food. 패스트푸드를 먹지 말아라.

The magician wears a <u>long</u> shirt. 그 마법사는 긴 셔츠를 입고 있다.

We have <u>enough</u> time and money. 우리는 충분한 시간과 돈을 가지고 있다.

The <u>early</u> worker will get a new job. 부지런한 노동자가 새 직업을 얻는다.

They subscribe to five <u>daily</u> newspapers. 그들은 다섯 개의 신문을 구독하고 있다.

My classmates read a weekly <u>high</u> teen magazine.

나의 클래스메이트는 주간 하이틴 잡지를 읽는다.

② 부사

My mom finished washing the dishes <u>fast</u>.	나의 엄마는 설거지하는 것을 끝냈다.
May you live <u>long</u>!	오래 사소서.
My son is old **enough** to marry.	나의 아들은 충분히 나이 먹어서 결혼할 수 있다.
Tomorrow morning, you must get up **early**.	너는 내일 아침에 일찍 일어나야 한다.
Water the flowers in the garden <u>daily</u>.	정원에 있는 꽃들에 매일 물 주어라.
The couple visit their parents <u>weekly</u>.	그 커플은 그들의 부모님을 매주 방문한다.

확인문제 5

다음 문장에서 굵은 글씨체의 단어가 형용사인지 부사인지를 구별하시오.

(01). We pay the rent **quarterly**.

(02). The bank pays interest **quarterly**.

(03). We distribute questionnaires to customers **quarterly**.

(04). You must achieve your **quarterly** sales target at all costs.

(05). Korea's **yearly** exports surpassed $250 billion.

(06). The manager has a **yearly** vacation.

(07). This flower is a **yearly** plant.

(08). This magazine is a **quarterly** publication.

(09). The newspaper is published **weekly**.

(10). The **weekly** magazine sell well.

(11). The Hankyoreh is a **daily** newspaper.

(12). The workers of the company get paid **daily**.

(13). How much do you save **monthly**?

(14). Legal Times is a **monthly** law magazine.

(15). **Finally**, it was the rabbit's turn to go to the lion.

(16). There are some 50,000 to 60,000 fires of unknown causes **yearly**.

B. 형용사와 부사로 쓰이며 −ly가 붙으면 추상적의미의 다른 뜻의 부사가 되는 단어들

−ly를 붙여서 다른 뜻의 부사를 만드는 단어도 있다.

	형용사	부사
right	옳은	정확히
rightly		당연히
high	높은	높이
highly		매우
wide	넓은	넓게
widely		대단히
hard	단단한	열심히, 심하게
hardly		※ 거의 ∼하지 않다.
near	가까운	가까이
nearly		거의
late	늦은	늦게
lately		최근에
most	대부분의	가장
mostly		대개
close	가까운	가까이
closely		면밀히
last	마지막의	마지막으로
lastly		최후로

Level UP

① 형용사

Look at that <u>high</u> building.   저 높은 빌딩을 보아라.

The furniture is very <u>hard</u>.   그 가구는 매우 단단하다.

They kept a <u>close</u> distance.   그들은 가까운 거리를 유지했다.

② 부사

Jump as <u>high</u> as possible.   가능한 한 높이 점프해라.

They sat down <u>close</u>.   그들은 가까이 앉았다.

Honor students study <u>hard</u>.   우등생들은 열심히 공부한다.

③ 추상적의미의 부사

It <u>hardly</u> rains in the desert.   사막에서는 결코 비가 내리지 않는다.

The natural resources are <u>highly</u> precious.   자연자원들은 매우 소중하다.

The detective looked into the case <u>closely</u>.   그 탐정은 치밀하게 그 사건을 조사했다.

확인문제 6

다음 문장에서 적절한 말을 (　　　) 안에서 고르시오.

(01). The train was (　　　) full.(near, nearly)

(02). We want to live (　　　) to the station.(near, nearly)

(03). The children were (　　　) amused.(high, highly)

(04). Babe Ruth threw the ball (　　　) into the air.(high, highly)

(05). The ball went (　　　) of the goal. (wide, widely)

(06). The farmers were (　　　) hit by the bad weather.(hard, hardly)

(07). The patients have (　　　) eaten anything nowadays.(hard, hardly)

(08). It's (　　　) believed that the government will lose the election. (wide, widely)

《정답과 해설 7P》

Study 03 횟수부사(빈도부사)

횟수부사는 얼마나 자주 발생하는가를 나타낸다.
always, usually, often, sometimes, <u>seldom/scarcely/hardly/rarely</u>, never가
있다.

횟수 부사의 위치

be동사나 조동사 다음에 온다. 그리고 일반동사 앞에 온다.

- be동사/조동사(can, will, should 등) V
- V 일반동사

- They are <u>always</u> happy.
- He will <u>always</u> win the game.
- Mom <u>often</u> praises me.

그들은 항상 행복하다.
그는 항상 게임에서 이길 것이다.
엄마는 가끔 나를 칭찬한다.

 확인문제 7

괄호 안의 단어를 알맞은 위치에 넣으시오.

(01). I will love you. (always)

(02). The professor is late.(always)

(03). The baby is sick.(sometimes)

(04). She stays home on Sunday. (usually)

(05). The boy was sick. (often)

(06). Men make mistakes. (often)

(07). What do you do in your free time? (usually)

(08). My friends go to school by bus. (usually)

(09). The boy comes home at ten o'clock at night. (often)

(10). The girls go to school by shuttle bus.(always)

(11). My girl friend play the piano at night.(sometimes)

(12). My husband forgets my phone number.(always)

(13). I clean the blackboard after a class.(never)

《정답과 해설 8P》

further study 형용사처럼 쓸 수 있는 것들

형용사와 마찬가지로 명사의 앞이나 뒤, 주어보충어, 목적어보충어 자리에서 명사를 꾸며 줄 수 있다.

- 형용사
- 전치사 + 명사
- to 동사원형
- 동사원형ing
- p.p(과거분사)
- 형용사절
  (who, whom, which, that, when, where, why, how 주어 + 동사~)

1. 형용사

• She poured <u>warm</u> milk into the bottle. 그녀는 따뜻한 우유를 병에 따랐다.

2. 전치사 + 명사

• The books <u>in the bookshelf</u> are all interesting. 책장에 있는 책들은 모두 재미있다.

3. to 동사원형

• The students have homework <u>to do</u>. 학생들은 해야 할 많은 숙제가 있다.

4. 동사원형ing

• I know the dancer <u>dancing</u> on the stage. 나는 무대에서 춤추고 있는 댄서를 안다.

5. p.p(과거분사)

- The <u>surprised</u> birds flew away.   놀란 새들이 날아갔다.

6. 형용사절 (접속대명사 who, whom,which, that/ 접속부사 when where why how)

- I have a friend <u>who always helps me</u>.   나는 나를 항상 돕는 친구를 가지고 있다.
- That is the store <u>which sell vegetables cheaply</u>.   저곳은 야채를 싸게 파는 가게이다.

 확인문제 8

다음 각 문장에서 형용사에 해당하는 단어·어구·어절을 말하시오.

(01). My favorite music is rock.

(02). SNS improves our quality of life.

(03). Others voice concern about its dangers.

(04). The butter in the bread spoiled his work.

(05). I had a traditional dish called tinolang manok.

(06). Direct contact can help us make true friendships.

(07). Social networking services create online communities.

(08). We can meet people who share our interests and activities.

(09). Social networking services are useful tools for connecting people.

(10). The information which you have on your social networking website is not safe.

(11). Foreign friends share my interest in music through these services.

(12). I have made a lot of friends who have the same taste in music.

〈정답과 해설 8P〉

further study 부사처럼 쓸 수 있는 것들

부사와 마찬가지로 동사, 형용사, 다른 부사, 문장전체를 꾸며 줄 수 있다.

- 부사
- 전치사+명사
- to 동사원형
- 동사원형ing
- p.p(과거분사)
- 부사절(as, because, if, though, after 주어+동사 ～, etc.)

1. 부사

- Fern came <u>slowly</u>.   Fern은 천천히 왔다.

2. 전치사 + 명사

- Fern peered <u>through the door</u>.   Fern은 문들 통해서 내다보았다.
- Tears ran <u>down her cheeks</u>.   눈물이 그녀의 뺨 아래로 흘러 내렸다.
- He poured water <u>into the cup</u>.   그는 물을 컵에 부었다.

3. to 동사원형

- The boys went to the lake <u>to swim</u>.   그 소년들은 수영하기 위하여 호수에 갔다.

4. 동사원형ing

- <u>Arriving at the store</u>, he bought some kinds of fruits.   그는 가게에 도착하여 몇가지 과일을 샀다.

5. p,p(과거분사)

- <u>Surprised at the news,</u> the people watched TV.　　　　국민들은 뉴스에 놀란 채, TV를 봤다.

6. 부사절(as, because, if, though, after, etc.)

- <u>Though he is poor,</u> he is very happy.　　　　그는 가난했지만 그는 매우 행복했다.
- <u>As the girl has no books,</u> she goes to the library everyday.

그 소녀는 어떠한 책도 없었기 때문에 매일 도서관에 간다.

확인문제 9

다음 각 문장에서 부사에 해당하는 단어·어구·어절을 모두 말하시오.

(01). Time is simply wasted.

(02). We swam in the sea.

(03). You could get into trouble.

(04). When they saw us, they welcomed us.

(05). The man hurried to door to look around.

(06). Many of them don't really care about me.

(07). We spend too much time on these services.

(08). Luckily, a man near the hospital read a message.

(09). When he came in, he would often chat for a while

(10). Information can be shared immediately through SNS.

(11). You always need to protect your personal information.

(12). Sitting down with jam and coffee, "Hello," said she.

〈정답과 해설 8P〉

Grammar in Reading

〈정답과 해설 30〉

1. 다음 문장에서 각각의 문장에서 주어진 (   ) 안의 단어를 알맞은 곳에 넣어 문장을 각각 쓰시오.

When Ms. Smith goes shopping, ⓐ <u>she makes a shopping list.(always)</u> When she eats out with her family, ⓑ <u>she uses coupons.(usually)</u> She collects cans, bottles and newspapers. She sells them to make money. ⓒ <u>She must be diligent.(always)</u>

01. ⓐ-
02. ⓑ-
03. ⓒ-

2. 다음 문장에서 ⓐ, ⓑ의 각각의 문장에서 주어진 (   ) 안의 단어를 알맞은 곳에 넣어 문장을 각각 쓰시오.

Hello, Dr. Green! I'm Jiho, and this is my dog, Mongsil.

I'm worried about her.
When I hold her, ⓐ <u>her body feels a little hot (always)</u>.

But she doesn't look sick.

She eats well and plays well, too. Is there something wrong with her?
OK. Let me take her temperature.

Don't worry. There's no problem with her. Our normal body temperature is about 36.5℃, but the temperature of a dog is higher than that.

ⓑ <u>It's between 38℃ and 39℃ (usually)</u>, so Mongsil's body is always warmer than your body. Mongsil is OK.

01. ⓐ-
02. ⓑ-

Grammar in Reading

《정답과 해설 8~9P》

3. 다음 글에서 사용된 단어가 형용사인지 부사인지 구별하여 쓰시오.

Weather words are used in ⓐ <u>many</u> ways. If a person makes everyone ⓑ <u>happy</u>, he or she is called a ray of sunshine. If someone runs ⓒ <u>fast</u>, he or she runs like the wind. When people save money for a bad time, they save for a ⓓ <u>rainy</u> day.

01. ⓐ-   02. ⓑ-   03. ⓒ-   04. ⓓ-

4. 다음 글에서 사용된 단어가 형용사인지 부사인지 구별하여 쓰시오.

Helen Keller was born in 1880. She became ⓐ <u>blind</u> and deaf when she was a baby. The world was ⓑ <u>very</u> dark and quiet for her. When Helen was seven, she met a ⓒ <u>great</u> teacher, Annie Sullivan. She taught her how to read and write. Two years later, she could read and write ⓓ <u>well</u>

01. ⓐ-   02. ⓑ-   03. ⓒ-   04. ⓓ-

5. 다음 글에서 사용된 단어가 형용사인지 부사인지 구별하여 쓰시오.

This morning I got up ⓐ <u>late</u> because I studied for the exam until 2 a.m. I had to hurry to catch the school bus. I missed it, so I was ⓑ <u>late</u> for school. I didn't even do ⓒ <u>well</u> on the exam. What a ⓓ <u>terrible</u> day!

01. ⓐ-   02. ⓑ-   03. ⓒ-   04. ⓓ-

〈정답과 해설 112〉

1. 다음 짝지어진 단어들의 관계가 다른 하나는?

01.
① happy – happily　　② bad – badly　　③ final – finally
④ calm – calmly　　⑤ friend – friendly

02.
① wool–woolly　　② love–lovely　　③ man – manly
④ gentle–gently　　⑤ ghost–ghostly

03.
① fair – fairly　　② soft – softly　　③ coward – cowardly
④ private – privately　　⑤ sudden – suddenly

04.
① order – orderly　　② nice – nicely　　③ clean – cleanly
④ total – totally　　⑤ remote – remotely

05.
① usual –usually　　② useful –usefully　　③ clear – clearly
④ soft – softly　　⑤ year – yearly

06.
① ghost – ghostly　　② body – bodily　　③ wool – woolly
④ beast – beastly　　⑤ slight – slightly

2. 다음 단어의 형용사형을 쓰시오, 그리고 형용사의 뜻을 쓰시오.

01. coward　　_____,　　_____

02. man　　_____,　　_____

03. hair　　_____,　　_____

04. fur　　_____,　　_____

정답과 해설 p.25

05. luck   _____, _____

06. cloud   _____, _____

07. rain   _____, _____

08. snow   _____, _____

09. sun   _____, _____

10. fog   _____, _____

3. 다음 형용사형 단어들의 뜻을 쓰고 부사형을 만드시오.

01. usual   _____, _____

02. useful   _____, _____

03. obvious   _____, _____

04. evident   _____, _____

05. ardent   _____, _____

06. sharp   _____, _____

07. personal   _____, _____

08. sly   _____, _____

09. unique   _____, _____

10. acute   _____, _____

11. keen   _____, _____

12. abundant _____ , _____

13. lucky _____ , _____

14. cruel _____ , _____

15. final _____ , _____

16. useful _____ , _____

17. peaceful _____ , _____

18. pure _____ , _____

19. abrupt _____ , _____

20. global _____ , _____

4. 다음 문장에서 굵은 글씨체의 단어가 형용사인지 부사인지를 구별하시오.

01 The man seems **friendly**

02. The library looked **orderly**.

03. The alien came **peacefully**.

04. The dictator appeared **cowardly**.

05. The team had a **lucky** chance.

06. The woman wears a **woolly** coat.

07. We can make our fate **free**.

08. The newspaper is **weekly**.

09. His card trick **really** surprised us.

10. The lion **angrily** asked the rabbit.

5. 다음 문장에서 굵은 글씨로 사용된 단어가 형용사로 사용되었는지 부사로 사용되었는지를 말하시오.

01. The player is the **fast** runner.

02. The player runs **fast**.

03. The bridge is very **long**.

04. My office is very **near**.

05. Let's go the **near** station.

06. My family live quite **near**.

07. The train was **late** on schedule.

08. We were **late** for a train.

09. My son returned in the **late** night.

10. The bus arrived fifteen minutes **late**.

11. You have to work **hard**.

12. My daughter studied **hard** to get 100 points.

13. It is **hard** to climb the mountain.

14. Those nuts are so **hard** to eat.

15. It rained **hard** about this time last year.

16. An **early** bird catches a worm.

17. Those who want to see the sunrise tomorrow get up **early**.

18. The boy knew the **right** answer to the questions.

19. The boy answered to the questions **right**.

20. The country has **long** been famous for its magnificent temples.

6. 다음 문장에서 굵은 글씨로 사용된 단어가 형용사로 사용되었는지 부사로 사용되었는지를 말하시오.

01. The company is **close** to my house.

02. My family sat together **close**.

03. When did you **last** see him?

04. "The Magic Flute" is Mozart's **last** opera.

05. Jenifer is the **last** woman I have expected to see here.

06. You've been working much too **hard**.

07. The citizens waited for the president for a **long** time.

08. This ice cream is as **hard** as rock.

09. There were some **hard** questions on the exam paper.

〈정답과 해설 p. 10〉

10. This mid-term math exam is really **hard** to solve.

11. The kites fly **high** in the sky.

12. If you eat **right** and exercise regularly, you can live a longer and happier life.

13. About 80 percent of the country is covered by **high** mountains.

14. The **high** cost of heating is an issue especially during winter.

15. A **wide** range of chemicals are being found in marine ecosystem.

16. "Open **wide**" said the dentist.

17. The Grand Canyon is 446 kilometers long and 29 kilometers **wide**.

18. This is the **most** comfortable hotel in this area.

19. The voters stayed up **late** to watch the election result on the television.

20. The **most** people doubt the announcement of the police investigation of election fraud.

7. 다음 우리말과 뜻이 같도록 주어진 단어들을 알맞게 배열하시오.

01. 그는 항상 다른 사람들에게 친절하다.
   (kind, other, he, to, always, is, people)
   → _____

02. 나는 토요일 오후에 자주 영화를 본다.
   (often, see, I, on, afternoon, a, Saturday, movie)
   → _____

03. 너의 부모님은 평소에 산책을 하시니?
   (walk, do, usually, go, a, your, for, parents)
   → _____

04. 그들은 방과 후에 항상 축구를 한다.
(always, they, play, soccer, after, school)

→ _____

05. 어머니는 대개 아침에 바쁘시다.
(usually, mother, busy, in, the, is, morning)

→ _____

06. 해는 항상 동쪽에서 뜬다.
(rise, the, the, in, sun, always, east)

→ _____

07. 문을 잠그는 것을 절대 잊지 마라.
(lock, forget, to, the, never, door)

→ _____

08. 그 회장은 회의에 결코 늦지 않는다.
(the, is, never, president, the, late, for, meeting)

→ _____

09. 한국에서는 여름에 항상 뜨겁다.
(it, hot, in, is, always in, summer, Korea)

→ _____

10. 나의 가족은 때때로 피크닉 간다.
(my, sometimes, go, a, family, on, picnic)

→ _____

Chapter

03

Making Sentences
문장의 형식

1형식 문장
주어+주어의 동사

신랑과 신부만으로 이루어진 가족처럼,
문장의 핵심구조가 '주어(신랑)+주어의 동사(신부)'형태로 이루어진 문장을
말한다.

• The wind shifts.	바람이 바뀌다.
• A mouse squeaked.	쥐가 찍찍 거렸다.
• The sun shines.	태양이 빛난다.
• The herb medicine works.	약초약이 효과가 있다.
• A rodent's face appeared.	설치류의 얼굴이 보였다.

CF   1형식 특별구조
'There + be동사 등 +주어' 형태에서 There는 주어가 아니고 말을 끌어내는 부사일 뿐이다.
주어는 동사 뒤에 온다.

There is wind by the sea.   바닷가에 바람이 있다.

확인문제 1

다음 주어 진 문장에 보기에서 동사를 골라 연결하여 각각 적절한 문장을 만들어보시오.

crawl shrieked roars lived moves falls sets blossom arrived fly

(01). Silence _____. (침묵이 흐른다.)

(02). The sun _____. (태양이 진다.)

(03). The flowers _____. (꽃이 핀다.)

(04). The train _____. (열차가 도착했다.)

(05). Butterflies _____. (나비들이 난다.)

(06). Ants _____. (개미가 긴다.)

(07). Tina _____. (비명소리를 질렀다.)

(08). The sea water _____. (바다물이 으르렁댄다.)

(09). The earth _____. (지구가 돈다)

(10). The old man _____. (노인이 살았다.)

《정답과 해설 101》

1형식 문장의 확장

⊙ 부사와 부사가 될 수 있는 '전치사+명사', 'to+동사원형'등이 와서 1형식문장을 확장 할 수 있다. 이 부사역할 하는 것들은 문장 맨 앞이나 뒤, 중간에도 올 수 있다.

- A mouse squeaked <u>on and on</u>.   쥐새끼가 계속 찍찍 거렸다.
- The sun shines <u>brightly</u>.   태양이 밝게 빛난다.
- The herb medicine works <u>to flu</u>.   약초약이 독감에 효과가 있다.
- A rodent's face appeared <u>on the screen</u>.   설치류의 얼굴이 스크린에 나타났다.

다음 주어진 1형식 문장을 보기에서 적절한 부사어구를 연결하여 적절한 문장으로 확장하시오.

over the flowers   around the sun   in the sea   at the station   on the ground   widely
between the man and his girlfriend   to be 99 years old   in the room, fiercely

(01). Silence falls _____. (그 남자와 그의 여자친구사이에서)

(02). The sun sets _____. (바다에서)

(03). The flowers blossom _____. (활짝)

(04). The train arrived _____. (역에)

(05). Butterflies fly _____. (꽃 위에서)

(06). Ants crawl _____. (땅위에서)

(07). Tina shrieked _____. (방안에서)

(08). The sea water roars _____. (거칠게)

(09). The earth moves _____. (태양 둘레에서)

(10). The old man lived _____. (99살이 되었다)

Study 02

2형식 문장
주어+주어의 동사+주어 보충어

'신랑+신부+신랑 닮은 아들' 형식의
'주어(신랑)+주어의 동사(신부)+주어 보충어(신랑 닮은 아들)' 형태의 문장을
말한다.

⊙ 대표적인 2형식 동사는 be동사이다. 또 look, seem, appear, sound, smell, taste, feel, get, come, fall, grow, become, keep, prove 등이다. 주어보충어는 명사, 형용사 등은 가능하지만 부사는 절대 올 수 없다.

- Her voice sounds sweet.   그녀의 목소리가 달콤하게 들린다.
- This medicine tastes bitter.   이 약은 쓴맛이 난다.

확인문제 3

다음 문장에서 밑줄에 알맞은 동사를 보기에서 골라 현재 형태로 넣으시오.

get   fall   keep   look   prove

(01). The actress _____ smart.

(02). The audience _____ angry.

(03). The students _____ asleep.

(04). The snakes _____ motionless.

(05). The rumor _____ true.

확인문제 4

다음 문장에서 틀린 문장을 찾아 올바로 고치시오.

(01). The seagulls fly low.

(02). The days grew longer.

(03). The sky grew dark.

(04). The weather turned colder.

(05). The child looks unhappily.

(06). He looked quite young.

(07). She looks beautifully.

(08). The sea seems deeply.

2형식 문장의 확장

⊙ 부사와 부사가 될 수 있는 '전치사＋명사', 'to＋동사원형' 등이 와서 2형식문장을 확장 할 수 있다. 이 부사역할 하는 것들은 문장 맨 앞이나 뒤, 중간에도 올 수 있다.

- Her voice sounds sweet <u>to me</u>.
- This medicine tastes bitter <u>to the patients</u>.
- Dad got angry <u>to be stuck for words</u>.

그녀의 목소리는 나에게 달콤하게 들린다.

이약은 환자들에게 쓰게 맛이 난다.

아빠는 화가 나서 말문이 막혔다.

🔍 확인문제 5

다음 문장에서 빈칸의 한글에 해당하는 말을 '전치사 + 명사', 'to동사원형' 등 형태로 넣으시오.

(01). (무대에서), the actress looks smart.

→ _____.

(02). (강당 안에서), the audience get angry.

→ _____.

(03). The students fell asleep (그것을 이해 할 수가 없었다)

→ _____.

Chapter 03 문장의 형식 **91**

Study 03 3형식 문장
주어+동사+목적어

'신랑+신부+ 신랑 닮지 않은 아들'구조처럼
'주어(신랑)+주어의 동사(신부)+목적어(신랑 닮지 않은 아들)'형태를
3형식이라고 한다.

- We followed Creepella.
- The singer married the actress.

우리는 크리펠라를 따랐다.
그 가수는 그 여배우와 결혼했다.

확인문제 6

다음 문장에서 밑줄에 알맞은 동사를 보기에서 골라 현재 형태로 넣으시오.

22 players   the dictator   the popular singer   the earth's future   the meeting   his room

(01). The robbers entered (   ). (강도들은 그의 방안에 들어갔다.)

(02). The believers support (   ). (신자들은 독재자를 지지한다.)

(03). The fans approached (   ). (팬들이 인기 가수에게 다가간다)

(04). Students discussed (   ). (학생들은 지구의 미래에 대해 토론했다)

(05). The animals attended (   ). (그 동물들은 회의에 참가했다.)

《정답과 해설 101P》

3형식 문장의 확장

⊙ 부사와 부사가 될 수 있는 '전치사+명사', 'to+동사원형'등이 와서 3형식문장을 확장 할 수 있다. 이 부사역할 하는 것들은 문장 맨 앞이나 뒤, 중간에도 올 수 있다.

• The detective investigated his room <u>closely</u>.	그 탐정은 그의 방을 면밀하게 조사했다.
• We followed Creepella <u>into the tomb</u>.	우리는 무덤 안으로 크리필라를 따라갔다.
• <u>In 2014</u>, the singer married the actress.	2014년에 그 가수는 그 여배우와 결혼했다.
• He entered the gym <u>to see the star player</u>.	그는 스타선수를 보기위하여 체육관에 들어갔다.

 확인문제 7

다음 문장에서 괄호 안에 알맞은 부사어구를 넣어서 3형식 문장을 확장하시오.

(01). The people support the president (즐겁게).

→ _____.

(02). The fans approached the popular singer (거리에서).

→ _____.

(03). The robbers entered his room (보석을 훔치기 위하여-steal jewelry).

→ _____.

(04). Students discussed the earth's future (지난주).

→ _____.

(05). The animals attended the meeting (숲속에서-forest).

→ _____.

<정답과 해설 102>

Study 04

4형식 문장
주어+주어의 동사+간접목적어+직접목적어

아들이 둘 있는 신랑과 신부의 가족으로 '신랑+신부+아들1+아들2' 형식이다.
'**주어(신랑)+주어의 동사(신부)+간접목적어(아들1)+직접목적어(아들2)**'
문장이다.

- Mom made me bread.
- My elder brother will buy me a car.

엄마는 나에게 빵을 만들어 주었다.
나의 형은 나에게 차를 사줄 것이다.

⊙ 4형식문장은 3형식문장으로 바꿀 수 있다. 3형식문장으로 바꿀 때, 간접목적어를 뒤로 뺀다. 간접목적어 앞에 전치사를 써준다. ask일 때 of를 써주고 buy, choose, make, find, get, cook일 때는 for, 나머지 offer, give, write, send 등은 to를 쓴다.

4형식: 주어 + 동사 + <u>간접목적어</u> + <u>직접목적어</u>

→ 3형식: 주어 + 동사 + <u>목적어</u> + <u>전치사(to, for, of, on)</u> 명사
- ask ··················· <u>of</u> 명사
- buy, choose, make, find, get, cook ···· <u>for</u> 명사
- give, send, tell, show, offer ·········· <u>to</u> 명사

- The boy asked him many questions.   그 소년은 그에게 많은 질문을 했다.
  → The boy asked many questions <u>of him</u>.

- She cooked her children pizza.   그녀는 그녀의 아이들에게 피자를 요리해 주었다.
  → She cooked pizza <u>for her children</u>.

- She gave me ice cream.   그녀는 나에게 아이스크림을 주었다.
  → She gave ice cream <u>to me</u>.

- John showed the boys a map.   존은 그 소년들에게 지도를 보여 주었다.
  → John showed a map <u>to the boys</u>.

확인문제 8

다음 문장에서 간접목적어와 직접목적어를 각각 쓰시오.

(01). Jessica bought me a Christmas card.

(02). Kevin made me a cookie house.

(03). Kevin gave Sally some cookies.

(04). Jessica showed him her new book.

(05). The applicant sent me his resume.

(06). Creepella gave us some ideas for Halloween costumes.

《정답과 해설 11P》

확인문제 9

다음 4형식 문장을 3형식으로 바꾸어 쓰시오.

(01). Mary told him the news.

→ _____.

(02). Mr. Kim teaches them English.

→ _____.

(03). My mother made me a pretty bag.

→ _____.

(04). Please get me some water.

→ _____.

(05). I'll lend you some money.

→ _____.

《정답과 해설 11P》

확인문제 10

다음 괄호 안에 주어진 단어 중 알맞은 것을 고르시오.

(01). I showed my heart (to , for) you.

(02). She made a scarf (to , for) me.

(03). He gave roses (to , of) the woman.

(04). Andy bought the camera (to , for) me.

(05). She told the secret (to , for) her friend.

(06). May I ask a favor (to , of) you?

4형식 문장의 확장

⊙ 부사와 부사가 될 수 있는 '전치사+명사', 'to+동사원형'등이 와서 4형식문장을 확장 할 수 있다. 이 부사역할 하는 것들은 문장 맨 앞이나 뒤, 중간에도 올수 있다.

- His brother gave me a present <u>yesterday</u>.　　　그의 형은 나에게 어제 선물을 보냈다.
- Mom made me bread <u>in the morning</u>.　　　엄마는 아침에 나에게 빵을 만들어 주었다.
- <u>Probably</u> my elder brother will buy me a car.　　아마도 나의 형은 나에게 차를 사줄 것이다.

확인문제 11

다음 문장에서 괄호 안에 알맞은 말을 넣어서 4형식 문장을 확장하시오.

(01). Our teacher sent our parents report cards (지난주).

(02). The applicant sent me his resume (얼마간의 정보를 얻기 위하여).

(03). (그때에) Creepella gave us some ideas for Halloween costumes.

Study 05

5형식 문장
주어+주어의 동사+목적어+목적어 보충어

신랑과 신부, 그리고 그들의 아들, 그 아들의 아들 즉 손자로 구성된'신랑+신부 +아들+아들 닮은 손자 '형태이다.
'주어(신랑)+주어의 동사(신부)+목적어(아들)+목적어보충어(아들 닮은 손자)' 형태의 문장이다.

5형식은 두 개의 '주어+동사'가 한 문장으로 합해 진 것이다.

1. 목적어 보충어가 'to 동사원형'

⊙ 문장의 동사가 시간차가 있는 미래성 동사일 때. 미래성 동사:want, would like, allow, expect, get, persuade, ask, enable 등

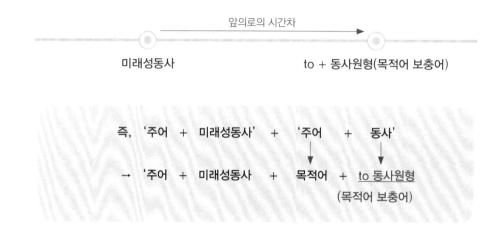

- He wants + I will major in music.
  → He wants me **to major** in music.

그는 내가 음악을 전공하기를 원한다.

- The old man allowed me **to use** his stick.
- Mom expects us **to come** back early.

한 노인은 내가 그의 지팡이를 사용하는 것을 허락했다.
엄마는 우리가 일찍 돌아올 것을 기대한다.

 확인문제 12

다음 문장에서 (   ) 안의 동사의 형태를 올바로 스시오.

(01). She wants me (clean) the room.

(02). Mom allowed you (play) soccer tomorrow.

(03). Our teacher would like us (study) hard.

(04). My grandparents expect me (call) on them often.

《정답과 해설 102》

2. 목적어 보충어가 '동사원형'

⊙ 문장의 동사가 시간차가 없는 동시성 동사일 때 [동시성 동사(사역동사와 지각동사)- let, make, have, see, look at, watch, notice, observe, hear, listen to, feel 등] 목적어 보충어는 동사원형이 온다. 이 때 목적어보충어'동사원형'은 주어의 동사의 시점과 같기 때문에 'to'를 쓰지 않고 '동사원형'을 쓴다.

동시성 동사(지각/사역동사)와 목적어 보충어의 동사원이 같은 시점이다.

- 사역동사: let, make, have
- 지각동사: see, look at, watch, notice, observe, hear, listen to, feel

즉, '주어 + 동시성동사' + '<u>주어</u> + <u>동사</u>'

→ '주어 + 동시성동사 + 목적어 + 동사원형
(목적어 보충어)

- The praise had + A whale danced.
  → The praise had a whale **dance**.

칭찬은 고래도 춤추게 한다고 한다.

- The boys heard + Someone cried out in the yard.
  → The boys heard someone **cry** out in the yard.

그 소년들은 누군가 뜰에서 외치는 것을 들었다.

- The teacher made us **clean** the window.

그 선생님은 우리가 창문을 청소하게 했다.

- We saw the man **dance** on the stage.

우리는 그 남자가 무대에서 춤추는 것을 보았다.

 확인문제 13

다음 문장에서 (   ) 안의 동사의 형태를 올바로 쓰시오.

(01). The owner let the man (use) the car.

(02). The people saw them (fight) in the street.

(03). The supporters heard a man (play) the guitar.

(04). The clerk of the shop let the customers (drink) water.

《정답과 해설 11P》

3. 목적어 보충어가 '동사원형ing'

⊙ 목적어가 진행 중일 때 (see, hear, find, leave 등)

즉, '주어 + 5형식동사' + '주어 + 동사'

→ '주어 + 5형식동사 + 목적어 + (be) 동사원형ing'
(목적어 보충어)

• The clerk found + A boy was stealing some books.
  → The clerk found a boy (be) **stealing** some books.

그 점원은 한 소년이 얼마간의 책을 훔치고 있는 것을 보았다.

• The spectators saw him **dancing** on the stage.   그 관중들은 그가 무대에서 춤추는 것을 보았다.
• The lonely boy found his friends **playing** soccer.

그 외로운 소년은 그의 친구들이 축구하고 있는 것을 보았다.

 확인문제 14

다음 문장에서 (   ) 안의 동사의 형태를 올바로 쓰시오.

(01). My friends watched the magician (dance) on the string.

(02). We found the players (fight) on the ground.

(03). The film director kept the audience (sit) in the cinema.

《정답과 해설 111》

4. 목적어 보충어가 'p.p-과거분사'

⊙ 목적어가 수동적인 관계 일 때

즉, '주어 + 5형식동사' + '<u>주어</u> + <u>동사</u>'

→ '주어 + 5형식동사 + 목적어 + <u>(be) p.p-과거분사</u>'

(목적어 보충어)

• We saw + The bag was stolen by the robber.

→ We saw the bag (be) **stolen** by the robber.   우리는 그 가방이 그 강도에 의해 훔쳐지는 것을 보았다.

• The robber saw his stolen goods **sold** in the market.

그 강도는 그의 도난당한 상품들이 시장에서 팔리는 것을 보았다.

• We had our house **painted** by the repairman.

우리는 우리의 집이 그 수리공에 의해 페인트칠 되도록 했다.

 확인문제 15

다음 문장에서 나타낼 때 (   ) 안의 동사의 형태를 올바로 쓰시오.

(01). The express bus driver saw a dog (run) on the highway.

(02). The doctor made the patient's eyes (close) for a moment.

(03). The runners saw some boys (play) on the playground.

(04). The driver had his car (repair) in the car center.

〈정답과 해설 11P〉

즉, '주어 + 동시성동사' + '<u>주어</u> + <u>동사</u>'

→ '주어 + 동시성동사 + 목적어 + (be) 명사'

(목적어 보충어)

- We found + The boy was a liar.
  →We found the boy (be) <u>a liar</u>.   우리는 그 소년이 거짓말쟁이라는 것을 알았다.

- The people call her <u>a dictator</u>.   국민들은 그녀를 독재자라고 부른다.
- The people elected him <u>a governor</u>.   국민들은 그를 주지사로 뽑았다.

 확인문제 16

다음 문장을 해석하시오.

(01). We call our baby 1004.

(02). Americans elected Obama their president.

(03). The advertiser chose Nancy Duke his company's model.

6. 목적어 보충어가 '형용사'

즉, '주어 + 동시성동사' + '주어 + 동사'

→ '주어 + 동시성동사 + 목적어 + (be) 형용사'
(목적어 보충어)

• The comedian made + The TV viewers were happy.
  →The comedian made the TV viewers (be) **happy**.   그 코미디언은 TV시청자들을 행복하게 만들었다.

• The magician got the kids **happy**.   그 마법사는 그 아이들이 행복하게 했다.
• The result of the exam made the students **sad**.   그 시험결과가 학생들이 슬프게 만들었다.

🔍 확인문제 17

다음 문장을 해석하시오.

(01). We found the boy sick.

(02). The accident made the people very sad.

(03). His victory got his friends happy.

〈정답과 해설 11P〉

further study

동시성 동사와 비슷하지만 다른 동사: find, leave, keep

1. 'to 동사원형'도 '동사원형'도 오지 않는다.

위 동사는 시간차가 없다는 면에서 see, hear, let, make, have 등 '동시성 동사'와 비슷하다. 시간차가 없으니 목적어 보충어자리에 'to 동사원형'은 오지 않는다. 또 이들 동사는 시간차가 없다는 면에서 '동시성동사'와 비슷하지만 '동사원형'은 쓰지 않는 차이점이 있다.

We found him (to) study English.(x)
They leave her (to) study math.(x)
Dad kept me (to) play basketball.(x)

2. 진행 중일 때 – '동사원형ing',가 온다.

We found him studying English. 우리는 그가 영어를 공부하고 있는 중임을 알았다.
The teacher keeps the students playing baseball. 그 선생님은 학생들이 야구를 하고 있는 중인 상태를 유지한다.
The woman left her son playing a game. 그 여자는 그녀의 아들이 게임을 하는 중인 상태로 남겨 놓았다.

3. 수동일 때 – 'p.p-과거분사'가 온다.

He left the cottage burned. 그는 그 오두막이 태워 진 채로 남겨 놓았다.
The man found the bird's wing broken. 그 남자는 그 새의 날개가 부러진 것을 발견했다.
The house owner keeps the window broken. 그 집주인은 창문이 깨어진 상태로 유지한다.

4. 형용사나 명사도 올 수 있다.

We find her happy. 우리는 그녀가 행복하다는 것을 발견한다.
Swimming keeps her slim. 수영은 그녀를 날씬하게 유지해 준다.
My friend found him a spy. 내 친구는 그가 스파이라는 것을 알았다.
She left the baby an orphan. 그녀는 그 아이를 고아로 남겨 놓았다.

Grammar in Reading

〈정답과 해설 11P〉

1. 다음 문장에서 각각 주어를 찾으시오.

ⓐ I am in a zoo, now. ⓑ I can see many animals. ⓒ The birds fly. ⓓ The fish swim in the water. ⓔ The dogs bark. ⓕ The horses run. ⓖ The elephants walk slowly. ⓗ The monkeys play in a tree. ⓘ The frogs jump on the pond. ⓙ The cats sleep. ⓚ A bear sits on a ball. ⓛ The ball rolls, and ⓜ the bear rolls. ⓝ The children smile at the bear.

01. ⓐ-	02. ⓑ-	03. ⓒ-	04. ⓓ-
05. ⓔ-	06. ⓕ-	07. ⓖ-	08. ⓗ-
09. ⓘ-	10. ⓙ-	11. ⓚ-	12. ⓛ-
13. ⓜ-	14. ⓝ		

2. 아래 글에서 각각의 문장이 몇 형식으로 쓰였는지 말하시오.

In some areas of the world, ⓐ the population is growing very fast. ⓑ This is true in parts of Africa, South America, and Asia. ⓒ Some countries in these areas are afraid of their future. Already, ⓓ these countries have serious problems. First of all, ⓔ food is a problem in many countries. ⓕ many people do not get enough to eat every day. ⓖ There are not enough houses or jobs. Also, ⓗ many people do not get education or medical care. ⓘ A larger population will make all these problems worse.

01. ⓐ-	02. ⓑ-	03. ⓒ-	04. ⓓ-
05. ⓔ-	06. ⓕ-	07. ⓖ-	08. ⓗ-
09. ⓘ-			

《정답과 해설 12P》

3. 아래 글에서 각각의 문장이 몇 형식으로 쓰였는지 말하시오.

These days, ⓐ parents seem to be always finding faults with us, the younger generation. ⓑ They criticize the clothes we wear, the music we listen to, our manners for the elderly. Maybe ⓒ they do have some reasons for these criticisms, but I am sure that they were not perfect when they were our age. So, please, parents, try to be a little more *tolerant of us. Then, ⓓ you will find that the majority of young people are kind and helpful.

01. ⓐ-   02. ⓑ-   03. ⓒ-   04. ⓓ-

4. 아래 글에서 각각의 문장이 몇 형식으로 쓰였는지 말하시오.

ⓐ Everyone bathes in a different way. ⓑ Most Americans seldom take a bath. They soap and rinse off under the shower. The English always take a bath. First, ⓒ they sit in a bathtub full of warm water. Then ⓓ they soap themselves, and finally, they rinse off the soap, all in the same water. ⓔ The Japanese, on the other hand, first wash with soap in the shower. Then they go and sit in a bathtub full of warm water for twenty minutes or more. ⓕ Later, others in the family use the same water to sit and relax in.

01. ⓐ-   02. ⓑ-   03. ⓒ-   04. ⓓ-
05. ⓔ-   06. ⓕ-

Grammar in Reading

〈정답과 해설 12~13P〉

5. 아래 글에서 각각의 문장이 몇 형식으로 쓰였는지 말하시오.

In the state of Washington, ⓐ there is a very unusual bridge which was built for squirrels. ⓑ The town of Longview has a very busy street. ⓒ Many cars use it every day. Squirrels were being killed as they tried to cross the street. ⓓ Mr. Peters built a bridge for the squirrels-one that would pass above the traffic. For years now, the squirrels have been able to cross safely from one side of the street to the other.

01. ⓐ-   02. ⓑ-   03. ⓒ-   04. ⓓ-

6. 아래 글에서 각각의 문장이 몇 형식으로 쓰였는지 말하시오.

ⓐ The ability to write good letters can be as useful as the ability to talk well. ⓑ In some ways letter writing can be even more useful to you. Because it helps make your social activities easy-often saves you much time and trouble. ⓒ The letter you write is your personal representative. It takes your place when you cannot be there. ⓓ It goes to the hospital to cheer a sick friend. ⓔ Letters can be one of the most powerful influences in your life.

*representative : 대리인

01. ⓐ-   02. ⓑ-   03. ⓒ-   04. ⓓ-
05. ⓔ-

7. 다음 글에서 어법상 맞지 않은 것을 모두 찾아 올바로 고치시오.

Has the smell of something ever made you to think of a spring day? Do some smells make you happily? Do others make you feeling relaxed? Believe it or not, smells can change the way we feel. Some of our basic emotions are linking to smell. For instance, scientists have found that the smell of the ocean or freshly baking cookies can revive very emotional memories. The smell of apples remind many people their homes. The smell of trees after a cool rain is calmed. The smell of peppermint excites us. The smell of lilies of the valley makes us feel relaxing.

《정답과 해설 13P》

1. 다음 문장이 각각 몇 형식 문장인지를 말하시오.

01. People rode on horses.
   [/   ]

02. Her eyes lighted brightly.
   [/   ]

03. All animals move around.
   [/   ]

04. This music sounds strange.
   [/   ]

05. Tears sprang to my eyes.
   [/   ]

06. My heart leaped with joy.
   [/   ]

07. The tree prepares for winter.
   [/   ]

08. The pizza smells delicious.
   [/   ]

09. The florist stared at me.
   [/   ]

10. Your girl friend looks beautiful.
   [/   ]

11. The Civil War began in 1861.
   [/   ]

12. The electronic tools seem good.
   [/   ]

《정답과 해설 13P》

13. Thousands of people died from cancer.
[/   ]

14. The seeds around us grow bigger.
[/   ]

15. Americans suffered from troubles inside the country.
[/   ]

2. 아래 문장들이 2형식문장인지 3형식 문장인지를 각각 구별하시오. 그리고 해석하시오.

01. The protest turned violent.
[/   ]

02. Mom stays awake all night.
[/   ]

03. My son washes the dishes.
[/   ]

04. The professor teaches German.
[/   ]

05. The king wants to conquer land.
[/   ]

06. You have no right to stay here.
[/   ]

07. Habits are like second nature.
[/   ]

08. Nicolette and his friends love soccer.
[/   ]

09. The volunteers want to help more.
    [/   ]

10. Computer addicts often skip meals.
    [/   ]

11. A person becomes uneasy or upset.
    [/   ]

12. The honor student studies math hard.
    [/   ]

13. Hellen wants to have a better friend.
    [/   ]

14. Dad brushes his teeth three times a day.
    [/   ]

15. The vegetable survives the heavy snow.
    [/   ]

3. 다음 두 문장이 같은 뜻이 되도록 빈칸에 알맞은 말을 쓰시오.

01. She gave me ice cream.
    = She gave ice cream _____ me.

02. She made me a scarf.
    = She made a scarf _____ me.

03. He gave the woman roses.
    = He gave roses _____ the woman.

04. Andy bought me the camera.
    = Andy bought the camera _____ me.

[정답과 해설 13~14P]

05. She told her friend the secret.
   = She told the secret _____ her friend.

06. May I ask you a favor.
   = May I ask a favor _____ you?

07. I showed you my heart.
   = I showed my heart _____ you.

08. John showed the boys a map.
   = John showed a map _____ the boys.

09. She cooked her children pizza.
   = She cooked pizza _____ her children.

10. The boy asked him many questions.
   = The boy asked many questions _____ him.

4. 다음 문장의 형식을 말하시오. 그리고 해석하시오.

01. Something is missing.
   [/   ]

02. Sarah lay laughing.
   [/   ]

03. There are bad storms.
   [/   ]

04. The sun rose higher.
   [/   ]

05. Your house seems lovely.
   [/   ]

06. The sheep ran in the field.
    [/   ]

07. The dogs rolled beside her.
    [/   ]

08. Caleb climbed the ladder.
    [/   ]

09. The sheep made Sarah smile.
    [/   ]

10. Caleb looked out the window.
    [/   ]

11. The stars blinked like fireflies.
    [/   ]

12. Papa lay back in the tall grasses again.
    [/   ]

13. The cows moved close to the pond.
    [/   ]

14. Caleb smiled at me across the table.
    [/   ]

15. Nick crept to lean against her knees.
    [/   ]

5. 다음 문장들의 문장의 형식을 각각 쓰시오. 그리고 해석하시오.

01. The project proved a failure.
    [/   ]

〈정답과 해설 11P〉

02. The building stood covered with dust.
[/   ]

03. Tony kept silent during the meeting.
[/   ]

04. They remained good friends all their lives.
[/   ]

05. Every minute counts.
[/   ]

06. The project seemed brilliant.
[/   ]

07. I found my car missing.
[/   ]

08. My elder brother found the weather cold in that country.
[/   ]

09. You must not leave the little boy alone.
[/   ]

10. Stress from work drove me crazy.
[/   ]

11. You look pale.
[/   ]

12. The police will tell you the truth.
[/   ]

13. The sun rises in the east.
[/   ]

14. The song sounds interesting.
   [/   ]

15. Her dad gave her a doll.
   [/   ]

6. 다음 문장들의 문장의 형식을 각각 쓰시오. 그리고 해석하시오.

01. The famous actor cried loudly.
   [/   ]

02. The actor left Seoul for Busan.
   [/   ]

03. We kept the window open.
   [/   ]

04. My husband is a computer programer.
   [/   ]

05. Mother bought me a good dress.
   [/   ]

06. The bank teller is an old friend of mine.
   [/   ]

07. The clerk helped me to finish the work.
   [/   ]

08. The native speaker teaches English at school.
   [/   ]

09. There are many flowers in the garden.
   [/   ]

10. This book cost me much money.
    [/   ]

11. The woman sent some flowers to me.
    [/   ]

12. The nurse made me wait for a long time.
    [/   ]

13. My father stopped smoking last year.
    [/   ]

14. Please keep the door close.
    [/   ]

15. My boyfriend bought me a gold ring.
    [/   ]

7. 다음 문장이 4형식 문장인지 5형식 문장인지를 말하시오. 그리고 각각 해석하시오.

01. Mary told him the news.
    [/   ]

02. Mr. Kim teaches them English.
    [/   ]

03. Jogging every morning keeps us healthy.
    [/   ]

04. My mother made me a pretty bag.
    [/   ]

05. Please get me some water.
    [/   ]

06. Comedic movies make me happy.
    [/   ]

07. I'll lend you some money.
    [/   ]

08. She asked her mother to fix the dress.
    [/   ]

09. The girls asked the singer a question.
    [/   ]

10. Please bring me a cup of tea.
    [/   ]

11. The man called me a bad name.
    [/   ]

12. The students sent a soldier a letter.
    [/   ]

13. My father bought me a used computer.
    [/   ]

14. The doctor advised me to exercise regularly.
    [/   ]

15. Jessica bought me a Christmas card
    [/   ]

16. My mother asked me to clean my room immediately.
    [/   ]

《정답과 해설 14P》

8. 다음 문장에서 목적어 보충어를 각각 쓰시오. 그리고 각각 해석하시오.

01. I want you to leave right now.
[/   ]

02. He told me to clean the room.
[/   ]

03. Gold arrows made people fall in love.
[/   ]

04. He asked me to wash his car.
[/   ]

05. She advised me to quit eating chocolate.
[/   ]

06. Plants make the air clean.
[/   ]

07. They'll let me stay for the whole summer.
[/   ]

08. Computers can help us (to) chat with others.
[/   ]

09. Let me tell you about my school days.
[/   ]

10. His wealth enabled him to go abroad.
[/   ]

11. The voters elected him president.
[/   ]

12. Visitors saw the fisher fishing in the river.
[/   ]

〔정답과 해설 111〕

13. Passengers had their luggage stolen in the bus.
[/   ]

14. The good idea makes the project productive.
[/   ]

15. My father allowed me to play computer games after dinner.
[/   ]

Chapter

04

Making Verbing
동사원형ing

Study 01 동사원형ing 만들기

'동사원형ing'는 동사를 명사(~하는 것), 형용사(진행 중, 감정유발, 상태지속), 부사로 사용하기 위하여 만든다

아래 특별한 경우를 제외하고 대부분의 경우		동사원형+ing	play → playing study → studying
특별한 경우	-e 로 끝나는 경우	-e를 없애고 +ing 다만 -ee로 끝나는 경우는 -ing만을 붙인다.	arrive → arriving make → making choose → choosing cf) -ee로 끝나는 단어 see → seeing agree → agreeing
	끝이 단모음+단자음	자음을 한 번 더 쓰고 + -ing cf>다만 2음절단어에서 앞에가 액센트 있는 경우는 -ing만 쓴다.	run → running begín → beginning cf> 앞에 액센트 있는 단어 énter → entering
	-ie 로 끝나는 경우	ie를 y로 바꾸고 + -ing	lie → lying

1. 일반적으로 '동사원형+ing'를 쓴다.

- meet → meeting
- find → finding
- watch → watching

2. 예외적인 경우

① -e로 끝나는 단어: e를 빼고 -ing를 붙인다.
- ride → riding
- give → giving
- believe → believing

② 발음이 '단모음+단자음'-마지막 자음을 겹치고 -ing를 붙인다.

a). 모든 1음절어
- stop → stopping
- jog → jogging

b). 2음절어 중에서 액센트가 뒤에 올 때
- occúr → occurring
- infér → inferring
- admít → admitting

다만 2음절단어에서 앞에가 액센트 있는 경우는 -ing만 쓴다.
- vísit → visiting

③ -ie로 끝나는 경우: ie를 y로 바꾸고 + -ing를 쓴다.
- die → dying

확인문제 1

다음 동사의 -ing 형태를 쓰시오.

(01). clean _____   (02). buy _____

(03). love _____   (04). hate _____

(05). allow _____   (06). dig _____

(07). sell _____   (08). run _____

(09). plant _____   (10). get _____

(11). drive _____   (12). find _____

(13). watch _____   (14). make _____

(15). have _____   (16). put _____

(17). hit _____   (18). throw _____

(19). become _____   (20). lose _____

《정답과 해설 15P》

🔍 확인문제 2

다음 동사의 –ing 형태를 쓰시오.

(01). argue _____   (02). discuss _____

(03). die _____   (04. lie _____

(05). laugh _____   (06). teach _____

(07). learn _____   (08). sing _____

(09). dance _____   (10). serve _____

(11). fight _____   (12). carry _____

(13). go _____   (14). pull _____

(15). use _____   (16). come _____

(17). take _____   (18). play _____

(19). bow _____   (20). breathe _____

《정답과 해설 15P》

Study 02 동사원형ing의 쓰임

동사가 명사, 형용사, 부사로 성격전환 하는 '동사원형ing'

'동사'는 일반적으로 주어 뒤에서 '주어의 동사'로서만 사용될 수 있다. 그래서 주어의 동사자리가 아닌 곳에서는 동사가 사용 될 수 없다.

다른 곳에서 사용하기 위해서는 동사의 성격을 바꿔 주어야 한다. 그 동사의 성격을 바꿔 줄 수 있는 방법 중 하나가 '동사원형ing'이다. 뒤에서 배울 'to 동사원형' 등도 있다.

'동사원형ing' 형태는 명사처럼 주어, 목적어, 보충어, 전치사 뒤에서 쓰이거나 형용사처럼 명사 앞이나 뒤, 주어보충어, 목적어보충어자리에서 사용된다. 문장전체를 꾸며주는 부사용법도 있다.

명사				형용사			
주어	목적어	보충어	전치사 뒤	명사 앞	명사 뒤	주어보충어	목적어보충어

1. 명사: ~하는 것

① 주어

- <u>Jogging</u> is a popular sport.　　　　　　　조깅은 인기 있는 스포츠이다.
- <u>Dieting</u> is the best way to lose weight.　　식사요법이 몸무게를 줄이는 최고의 방법이다.

② 목적어
- I do like **being** a doctor. 나는 의사가 되는 것을 좋아한다.
- My eyes do not need **testing**, Charlie. 나의 눈은 테스트되어질 필요가 없어, Charlie.

③ 주어보충어
- My bad habit was **biting my fingernails**. 나의 나쁜 습관이 손가락을 물어 뜯는 것이다.
- My brother's hobby is **playing computer games**. 나의 형의 취미는 컴퓨터게임을 하는 것이다.

④ 전치사 뒤
- She is good at **playing the piano**. 그녀는 피아노 연주를 잘한다.
- Mom objected to **doing the work**. 엄마는 일을 하는 것을 반대한다.
- He is afraid of **making mistakes**. 그는 실수하는 것을 두려워한다.

 확인문제 3

다음 각각의 문장의 주어자리에 사용된 동사원형ing에 유념하여 해석하시오.

(01). <u>Sweating</u> makes you lose weight.

→ _____

(02). <u>Using a cell phone</u> is not allowed here.

→ _____

(03). <u>Torturing a human being</u> is intrinsically wrong.

→ _____

(04). <u>Watching a baby grow up</u> was a fascinating experience.

→ _____

(05). <u>Studying music and language</u> has a lot in common.

→ _____

(06). <u>Running one kilometer</u> uses more energy than walking one.

→ _____

(정답과 해설 15P)

 확인문제 4

다음 각각의 문장의 목적어자리에 사용된 동사원형ing에 유념하여 해석하시오.

(01). Cathy likes <u>walking alone</u>.

    → _____

(02). My grandfather enjoys <u>playing golf</u>.

    → _____

(03). My mother doesn't like <u>playing computer games</u>.

    → _____

(04). Have you finished <u>reading the fairy tale</u>, Cathy?

    → _____

(05). He loved <u>learning more than anybody else</u>.

    → _____

(06). The government considered <u>raising tax on cigarettes</u>.

    → _____

〈정답과 해설 15P〉

확인문제 5

다음 각각의 문장의 주어보충어자리에 사용된 동사원형ing에 유념하여 해석하시오.

(01). The only purpose of my writing is <u>telling the truth.</u>

    → _____

(02). One key to survival is <u>having more roots than branches</u>.

    → _____

〈정답과 해설 15P〉

다음 각각의 문장의 전치사 뒤 자리에 사용된 동사원형ing에 유념하여 해석하시오.

(01). She went out without __saying__ anything.

   → _____

(02). I'm afraid of __talking__ in front of my class.

   → _____

(03). You must weigh right after __exercising__.

   → _____

(04). Hana has a great interest in __singing__ and __dancing__.

   → _____

(05). Try 20 minutes of aerobic activity, such as __running__ or __dancing__.

   → _____

(06). They tested their skills at __throwing__ a basketball through a hoop..

   → _____

2. 형용사: ~하고 있는(진행중), 감정유발, 상태지속

형용사는 명사 앞이나 뒤, 주어보충어. 목적어 보충어자리에 사용할 수 있다.

진행의 의미

① 명사 앞

- The __singing__ woman is my wife.   노래하고 있는 그 여자는 나의 아내이다.
- The __swimming__ children are 9 years old.   그 수영하고 있는 아이들은 9살 먹었다.

② 명사 뒤

- The woman __swimming__ in the pool is my sister.   수영장에서 수영하고 있는 나의 누이이다.
- The children __singing__ in a chorus are 6 grades in my school.

     코러스로 노래하고 있는 아이들은 나의 학교 6학년들이다.

③ 주어보충어(일반적으로 시제에서 진행형이라고 한다.)

과거   현재   미래

a). 현재 진행형

- They are <u>looking</u> around in the car.
- The family are <u>walking</u> for a day.

그들은 차안에서 구경하고 있는 중이다.
그 가족들은 하루 동안 걷고 있는 중이다.

b). 과거 진행형

- Three men were <u>traveling</u> across the desert.
- Her parents were <u>sitting</u> by her hospital bed.

세 남자들은 사막을 가로질러 여행하고 있는 중이다.
그녀의 부모는 병원침대에서 앉아 있는 중이었다.

c). 미래 진행형

- My uncle will be <u>jogging</u> at lunchtime tomorrow.

나의 삼촌은 내일 점심시간에 조깅하고 있는 중일 것이다.

- The kids will be <u>writing</u> down their goals next class.

아이들은 다음수업에서 그들의 목표를 쓰고 있는 중일 것이다.

④ 목적어보충어

- The soldiers watched the man <u>driving</u> away.
- The fisher man saw the ship <u>leaving</u> for an island.

군인들은 그 남자가 차를 운전하여 떠나고 있는 것을 보았다.
어부는 배가 섬을 향하여 떠나는 것을 보았다.

🔍 확인문제 7

다음 문장에서 사용된 '동사원형ing'는 진행의 뜻을 나타내는 형용사 역할 한다. 밑줄 그은 '동사원형ing'가 꾸며주는 명사를 쓰고 각각 해석하시오. (참고-형용사는 뒤에 오는 명사, 앞에 오는 명사, 주어, 목적어를 꾸며준다.)

(01). The girl <u>drawing</u> cartoons is my cousin.

(,   )

(02). We saw a <u>singing</u> bird in the zoo.

(,   )

(03). The boys are <u>playing</u> soccer.

(,   )

(04). We saw the girl <u>crying</u> in the room.

(,   ) 《정답과 해설 15P》

Plus UP

동사원형ing는 진행이외에 감정유발. 상태지속을 나타내는 경우도 있다.

감정유발　　～ 하게 하는

① 명사 앞

- Watching the scene was a <u>fascinating</u> experience.　　그 장면을 보는 것은 환상적인 경험이다.

② 명사 뒤

- Let's find a game <u>amazing</u> to us.　　우리들에게 놀라운 게임을 찾아보자.

③ 주어보충어

- The scenery is <u>amazing</u>.　　그 장면은 놀랍다.

④ 목적어보충어

- We found the movie <u>amazing</u> to girls.

우리는 그 영화가 소녀들에게 놀라게 한다는 것을 알았다.

 확인문제 8

다음 문장에서 사용된 '동사원형ing'는 '감정유발'의 뜻을 나타내는 형용사 역할 한다. '동사원형ing'가 꾸며주는 명사를 찾아 쓰고 각각 해석하시오. (참고-형용사는 뒤에 오는 명사, 앞에 오는 명사, 주어, 목적어를 꾸며준다.)

(01). I found his words <u>moving</u>.

　　(　　　　　　,　　　　　　　　　　　　　　)

(02). The play was <u>touching</u>.

　　(　　　　　　,　　　　　　　　　　　　　　)

(03). They heard the <u>shocking</u> news.

　　(　　　　　　,　　　　　　　　　　　　　　)

(04). This is the news <u>surprising</u> to all Koreans.

　　(　　　　　　,　　　　　　　　　　　　　　)

《정답과 해설 15P》

상태지속 ～하는

① 명사 앞

- My son found the **missing** dog.   나의 아들은 그 실종된 개를 찾았다.

② 명사 뒤

- This is the passage **leading** to the secret room.   이것은 비밀의 방으로 연결된 통로이다.
- That is the tree house **belonging** to the leader of the tribe.   저것은 그 부족의 리더에 속하는 나무집이다.

③ 주어보충어

- A great many stars are **shining** in the sky.   굉장이 많은 별들이 하늘에서 빛나고 있다.
- Her lips are **shaking** a little.   그녀의 입술은 약간 떨리고 있다.

④ 목적어보충어

- Tina found a garden with flowers **blooming**.   티나는 꽃이 있는 정원이 꽃이 만발하고 있는 것을 알았다.
- James saw his friends **dancing** on the stage.   제임스는 그의 친구들이 무대에서 춤추고 있는 것을 보았다.

확인문제 9

다음 문장에서 사용된 '동사원형ing'는 '상태지속'의 뜻을 나타내는 형용사 역할 한다. 밑줄 그은 '동사원형ing'가 꾸며주는 명사를 찾아쓰고 각각 해석하시오. (참고-형용사는 뒤에 오는 명사, 앞에 오는 명사, 주어, 목적어를 꾸며준다.)

(01). Some monkeys are **missing**.

(,   )

(02). The **missing** book is my father's.

(,   )

(03). Do you know the man **wearing** a red shirt?

(,   )

(04). I could see him **lying** in the bed.

(,   )

《정답과 해설 15P》

Level UP

'동사원형ing+명사'에서 '**동사원형ing**'

형용사용법과 명사용법 둘 중 하나로 쓰인다. '동사원형ing+명사'는 일반적으로 '～하고 있는 진행중'이나 '～하게 하는 감정유발'등을 나타내는 경우는 형용사용법이다.

a <u>living</u> man	살고 있는 남자
a <u>fishing</u> old man	낚시질 하고 있는 노인
a <u>frying</u> cook	볶고 있는 요리사
a <u>training</u> runner	훈련하고 있는 달리기 선수
a <u>washing</u> soldier	세탁하고 있는 군인

하지만 '명사 for 동사원형ing'(～를 위한 명사)를 간단히 하기 위하여 for 뒤의 '동사원형ing' 가 앞으로 넘어온 경우는 명사용법이다. 원래 전치사 for다음에 온 경우는 전치사 for의 목적어 이었기 때문이다.

a <u>living</u> room (←a room <u>for</u> living) 거실

a <u>fishing</u> rod (←a rod <u>for</u> fishing) 낚시 대

a <u>frying</u> pan (←a pan <u>for</u> frying) 후라이팬

a <u>training</u> center (←a center <u>for</u> training) 훈련센터

a <u>washing</u> machine (← a machine <u>for</u> washing) 세탁기

 확인문제 10

다음 '동사원형ing +명사'에서 밑줄 그은 '동사원형ing'가 형용사 용법인지 명사용법인지를 구별하시오.
그리고 각각 뜻을 쓰시오.

(01). ⓐ a fishing rod　　　　　　　＿＿＿＿＿＿,　＿＿＿＿＿＿＿＿＿
　　　ⓑ a fishing boy　　　　　　　＿＿＿＿＿＿,　＿＿＿＿＿＿＿＿＿

(02). ⓐ a training runner　　　　　＿＿＿＿＿＿,　＿＿＿＿＿＿＿＿＿
　　　ⓑ a training center　　　　　＿＿＿＿＿＿,　＿＿＿＿＿＿＿＿＿

(03). ⓐ a frying cook　　　　　　　＿＿＿＿＿＿,　＿＿＿＿＿＿＿＿＿
　　　ⓑ a frying pan　　　　　　　＿＿＿＿＿＿,　＿＿＿＿＿＿＿＿＿

(04). ⓐ a washing machine　　　　＿＿＿＿＿＿,　＿＿＿＿＿＿＿＿＿
　　　ⓑ a washing woman　　　　　＿＿＿＿＿＿,　＿＿＿＿＿＿＿＿＿

(05). ⓐ a swimming girl　　　　　＿＿＿＿＿＿,　＿＿＿＿＿＿＿＿＿
　　　ⓑ a swimming pool　　　　　＿＿＿＿＿＿,　＿＿＿＿＿＿＿＿＿

(06). ⓐ a sleeping baby　　　　　＿＿＿＿＿＿,　＿＿＿＿＿＿＿＿＿
　　　ⓑ a sleeping bag　　　　　　＿＿＿＿＿＿,　＿＿＿＿＿＿＿＿＿

(07). ⓐ a walking stick　　　　　　＿＿＿＿＿＿,　＿＿＿＿＿＿＿＿＿
　　　ⓑ a walking traveller　　　　＿＿＿＿＿＿,　＿＿＿＿＿＿＿＿＿

(08). ⓐ a shopping mall　　　　　＿＿＿＿＿＿,　＿＿＿＿＿＿＿＿＿
　　　ⓑ a shopping lady　　　　　＿＿＿＿＿＿,　＿＿＿＿＿＿＿＿＿

(09). ⓐ a smoking room　　　　　＿＿＿＿＿＿,　＿＿＿＿＿＿＿＿＿
　　　ⓑ a smoking actor　　　　　＿＿＿＿＿＿,　＿＿＿＿＿＿＿＿＿

(10). ⓐ a living room　　　　　　　＿＿＿＿＿＿,　＿＿＿＿＿＿＿＿＿
　　　ⓑ a living man　　　　　　　＿＿＿＿＿＿,　＿＿＿＿＿＿＿＿＿

〈정답과 해설 16P〉

further study   부사용법

'동사원형ing'가 문장 맨 앞이나 뒤, 혹은 문장 중간에 와 문장전체를 꾸며준다. 원인(~ 때문에), 조건, 시간, 동시동작(~하면서), 연속동작(~하고 나서 그리고), 상황상관없음(~일지라도)을 표현한다. 이 '동사원형ing'부사절 중 원인, 조건, 시간, 동시동작, 상황상관없음에 해당하는 문장이 간단히 된 것이다.

1. 원인

- Studying hard, he passed the exam.

  (=As he studied hard, he passed the exam.)

  그는 열심히 공부했기 때문에 시험에 합격했다.

- Knowing him well, I couldn't believe his story.

  (=Because I knew him well, I couldn't believe his story.)

  나는 그를 잘 알았기 때문에 그의 이야기를 믿을 수 없었다.

2. 조건

- Opening the box, you will find something surprising.

  (= If you open the box, you will find something surprising.)

  네가 상자를 열면 놀라운 무엇인가를 발견할 것이다.

3. 시간

- Meeting Hana at the bookstore, I went back home.

  (= After I met Hana at the bookstore, I went back home.)

  서점에서 하나를 만난 후에 나는 집에 돌아갔다.

- Listening to the radio, Tom looked at the pictures.

  (= While Tom listened to the radio, he looked at the pictures.)

  Tom은 라디오를 듣는 동안 사진들을 보았다.

4. 동시동작

- Cooking in the kitchen, Kelly sang some pop songs.
  (=As Kelly cooked in the kitchen, she sang some pop songs.)
  Kelly는 요리하는 동안 팝송을 불렀다.

5. 연속동작

- I entered my room, turning on TV.
  (=I entered my room, and it turned on TV.)
  나는 방안에 들어갔다, 그리고 TV를 켰다.
- This train leaves Daejeon at 9:00, arriving in Busan at 11:00.
  (= This train leaves Daejeon at 9:00 and (it) arrives in Busan at 11:00.).
  이 열차는 9시에 대전을 떠나 부산에 11시에 도착한다.

6. 상황상관없음

- Not being old enough, he is very wise and thoughtful.
  (=Although he is not old enough, he is very wise and thoughtful.)
  그가 충분히 나이 먹지 않았으나 그는 매우 현명하고 사려 깊다.

 확인문제 11

아래 문장에서 밑줄 그은 '동사원형ing'부분에 유의하여 원인(Because~ 때문에), 조건(If~이라면), 시간(When~했을 때, After ~한 후에), 동시동작(As ~하면서), 연속동작(and ~해서 ~하다), 상황 상관없음(양보-Though-~일지라도)중 하나로 적절하게 해석하시오.

(01). **Failing** in the job interview, I returned to university.

    → _____

(02). **Checking** the car, the policeman found the wheel broken.

    → _____

(03). **Crossing** the street in this intersection, kids must be careful.

→ _____

(04). **Feeling** confident, Susie asked for a salary raise.

→ _____

(05). **Knowing** the password, the criminal could access the internet.

→ _____

(06). Not **knowing** the password, the investigator couldn't access the internet.

→ _____

(07). **Exercising** very much, the player gains weight.

→ _____

(08). **Taking** the train, you will get in Seoul sooner.

→ _____

(09). **Turing** to the left, you will find the gas station.

→ _____

(10). **Hearing** the scream, the house owner ran to the window.

→ _____

(11). **Eating** very much, the patient loses weight.

→ _____

(12). **Smiling** to the reporters, the president couldn't hide his worries.

→ _____

Grammar in Reading

《정답과 해설 16P》

1. 아래 글에서 어법상 맞지 않는 것을 찾아 올바로 고치시오.

Now many people ride bikes. Bicycles are slower than cars, but ride a bike is great exercise. It helps you stay healthy. Also, bike riding is a way save the Earth. It doesn't make the air dirty.

2. 아래 글에서 어법상 맞지 않는 것을 찾아 올바로 고치시오.

Many people like live in a city. People in the city can go anywhere by bus, taxi or subway. There are many big stores in the city. People can often enjoy movies and concerts, too. But live in the country also has good points.

Grammar in Reading

〈정답과 해설 17P〉

3. 위 글의 밑줄 친 <u>Saying</u>과 쓰임이 다른 것은?

People sometimes help us. When they hear "thank you," they will be happy and will want to help you again. When your friend gives you a hand, you must not forget to say "thank you."

<u>Saying</u> "please" is polite. For example, you may want water in a restaurant.
You can say to your server, "May I have a glass of water?" Now, add the simple word "please" and say, "May I have a glass of water, please?" You are sure to get good service."

01. We enjoyed <u>walking</u> in the forest with my family.
02. Please stop <u>worrying</u> about your future now.
03. The passengers are <u>shaking</u> hands each other.
04. Minho's hobby is <u>collecting</u> old coins.
05. <u>Making</u> a snowman is a lot of fun.

4. 아래 글에서 밑줄 그은 <u>Playing</u> 및 <u>working</u>과 쓰임이 같지 않은 것은?

In the evening, Minho plays a video game with his pet robot. He has two robots. One is Gamey, the pet robot, and the other is Homey, the household
Homey likes to clean the rooms and make the bed for Minho. <u>Playing</u> with Gamey is exciting, and <u>working</u> with Homey is a lot of fun. After a busy day, he falls asleep and flies to Mars in his dream.

01. Thank you for <u>helping</u> us in many ways.
02. Laura finished <u>writing</u> a paper this morning.
03. One of Tony's hobbies was <u>collecting</u> stamps.
04. <u>Becoming</u> a successful actor is not easy.
05. She gave some cookies to the <u>crying</u> baby.

Grammar in Reading

《정답과 해설 17~18P》

5. 다음 밑줄 친 ⓐ, ⓑ, ⓒ의 동사원형ing 들과 쓰임이 같은 것을 모두 고르시오.

Now, listen to his presentation.

Nowadays, it is ⓐ <u>becoming</u> more common to hear about foreigners ⓑ <u>learning</u> Korean. In fact, Korean is no longer just for Koreans. More and more people around the world are ⓒ <u>learning</u> Korean. Some people learn Korean to study or work in Korea. Others learn it because they are interested in Korean popular culture such as Korean dramas and Korean pop songs.

01. Karl enjoys <u>collecting</u> stamps.
02. My father is <u>going</u> to the library.
03. Her job is <u>teaching</u> English.
04. Ann finishes <u>cleaning</u> and sits.
05. Hurry up! Everybody is <u>waiting</u> for you.
06. Are you <u>using</u> this computer now?
07. Look at the <u>swimming</u> boy.
08. The <u>smoking</u> man is my father.
09. <u>Jogging</u> is good for your health.
10. <u>Driving</u> a car too fast is dangerous.

6. 아래 밑줄 친 ⓐ, ⓑ의 동사원형ing 들과 쓰임이 같은 것을 모두 고르시오.

Most runners in the Antarctic Ice Marathon do not set any time goal. Just ⓐ <u>finishing</u> the race safely is their main goal. The most difficult part is the freezing wind. Temperatures often drop to −40℃. Also, ⓑ <u>running</u> on snow and ice is really tough.

01. They are <u>talking</u> under the tree.
02. I know the girl <u>standing</u> there.
03. <u>Smoking</u> cigarettes is bad for you.
04. Look at the <u>sleeping</u> children over there.
05. The girls are <u>sitting</u> in the shade.
06. He has to avoid <u>eating</u> unhealthy food.
07. <u>Getting</u> enough sleep is very important.
08. I saw a boy <u>dancing</u> in front of people.
09. They are <u>reading</u> the class newspaper.
10. My job is <u>taking</u> care of disabled children.

《정답과 해설 181》

1. 다음 동사를 명사나 형용사, 부사로 사용할 수 있는 '동사원형ing'형태를 쓰시오. 또 각 동사의 뜻을 쓰시오.

01. carry   _____ ,   _____

02. turn   _____ ,   _____

03. bring   _____ ,   _____

04. choose   _____ ,   _____

05. watch   _____ ,   _____

06. enter   _____ ,   _____

07. cut   _____ ,   _____

08. eat   _____ ,   _____

09. make   _____ ,   _____

10. wonder   _____ ,   _____

11. lie   _____ ,   _____

12. lay   _____ ,   _____

13. wander   _____ ,   _____

14. feel   _____ ,   _____

15. elect   _____ ,   _____

16. close   _____ ,   _____

17. mention   _____ ,   _____

ELECTION DAY

(정답과 해설 (8P))

18. pray   _____ , _____

19. try   _____ , _____

20. die   _____ , _____

21. worry   _____ , _____

22. await   _____ , _____

23. obey   _____ , _____

24. comply   _____ , _____

25. admire   _____ , _____

2. 다음 단어들의 뜻과 동사를 명사나 형용사, 부사로 사용할 수 있는 '동사원형ing'형태를 쓰시오.

01. stay   _____ , _____

02. print   _____ , _____

03. say   _____ , _____

04. join   _____ , _____

05. wait   _____ , _____

06. shake   _____ , _____

07. take   _____ , _____

08. mean   _____ , _____

09. visit   _____ , _____

〈정답과 해설 18P〉

10. kill   _____ ,   _____

11. travel   _____ ,   _____

12. think   _____ ,   _____

13. walk   _____ ,   _____

14. hunt   _____ ,   _____

15. meet   _____ ,   _____

16. run   _____ ,   _____

17. stop   _____ ,   _____

18. swim   _____ ,   _____

19. reduce   _____ ,   _____

20. decrease   _____ ,   _____

21. discover   _____ ,   _____

22. introduce   _____ ,   _____

23. recommend   _____ ,   _____

24. interview   _____ ,   _____

25. interfere   _____ ,   _____

《정답과 해설 18P》

3. 다음 동사의 3인칭 단수 현재형, 과거 및 p.p-과거분사형, 동사원형ing을 쓰시오.그리고 단어의 뜻을 쓰시오.

<blockquote>3인칭 단수현재형,　　과거형,　　p.p-과거분사형,　동사원형 ing,　　　뜻</blockquote>

01. miss ＿＿＿＿, ＿＿＿＿, ＿＿＿＿, ＿＿＿＿, ＿＿＿＿

02. make ＿＿＿＿, ＿＿＿＿, ＿＿＿＿, ＿＿＿＿, ＿＿＿＿

03. teach ＿＿＿＿, ＿＿＿＿, ＿＿＿＿, ＿＿＿＿, ＿＿＿＿

04. become ＿＿＿＿, ＿＿＿＿, ＿＿＿＿, ＿＿＿＿, ＿＿＿＿

05. study ＿＿＿＿, ＿＿＿＿, ＿＿＿＿, ＿＿＿＿, ＿＿＿＿

06. play ＿＿＿＿, ＿＿＿＿, ＿＿＿＿, ＿＿＿＿, ＿＿＿＿

07. cry ＿＿＿＿, ＿＿＿＿, ＿＿＿＿, ＿＿＿＿, ＿＿＿＿

08. buy ＿＿＿＿, ＿＿＿＿, ＿＿＿＿, ＿＿＿＿, ＿＿＿＿

09. hurry ＿＿＿＿, ＿＿＿＿, ＿＿＿＿, ＿＿＿＿, ＿＿＿＿

10. change ＿＿＿＿, ＿＿＿＿, ＿＿＿＿, ＿＿＿＿, ＿＿＿＿

11. finish ＿＿＿＿, ＿＿＿＿, ＿＿＿＿, ＿＿＿＿, ＿＿＿＿

12. jump ＿＿＿＿, ＿＿＿＿, ＿＿＿＿, ＿＿＿＿, ＿＿＿＿

13. relax ＿＿＿＿, ＿＿＿＿, ＿＿＿＿, ＿＿＿＿, ＿＿＿＿

14. wash ＿＿＿＿, ＿＿＿＿, ＿＿＿＿, ＿＿＿＿, ＿＿＿＿

15. reach ＿＿＿＿, ＿＿＿＿, ＿＿＿＿, ＿＿＿＿, ＿＿＿＿

16. destroy ＿＿＿＿, ＿＿＿＿, ＿＿＿＿, ＿＿＿＿, ＿＿＿＿

17. defend ＿＿＿＿, ＿＿＿＿, ＿＿＿＿, ＿＿＿＿, ＿＿＿＿

〈정답과 해설 101〉

18. rely　　　　_____, _____, _____, _____, _____

19. match　　　_____, _____, _____, _____, _____

20. commit　　_____, _____, _____, _____, _____

21. refer　　　_____, _____, _____, _____, _____

22. share　　　_____, _____, _____, _____, _____

4. 다음 문장에서 동사원형ing가 '명사용법'으로 쓰였는지 '형용사 용법'으로 쓰였는지를 구별하시오. 그리고 각각 해석하시오.

01. Look at the flying bird.
　　(　　　　　　,　　　　　　　)

02. Birds are singing.
　　(　　　　　　,　　　　　　　)

03. They saw him running fast.
　　(　　　　　　,　　　　　　　)

04. Suji thinks that drawing cartoons is fun.
　　(　　　　　　,　　　　　　　)

05. The boy is running in the garden.
　　(　　　　　　,　　　　　　　)

06. My father enjoys taking a walk every morning.
　　(　　　　　　,　　　　　　　)

07. What do you mean by nodding your head up and down?
　　(　　　　　　,　　　　　　　)

08. The girl looking at the painting is my friend.
　　(　　　　　　,　　　　　　　)

《정답과 해설 19P》

09. First, I'd like to thank you for coming today.
  (,   )

10. Watching movies makes me happy.
  (,   )

11. Alice is afraid of walking across the bridge.
  (,   )

12. I enjoy hanging out with other people.
  (,   )

13. The boy shaking hands with him is my friend.
  (,   )

14. I think your problem is eating too little.
  (,   )

15. The woman lying on the grass is my aunt.
  (,   )

16. Look at the dog playing with a ball.
  (,   )

17. Sora finished doing the dishes.
  (,   )

18. He stood looking as stupid as he could.
  (,   )

19. Going to bed early is important for children.
  (,   )

20. Don't you know that smoking is bad for your health?
  (,   )

memo.

Chapter

05

To Verb

동사를 성격전환하는
'to 동사원형'

'To 동사원형'의 쓰임

'to 동사원형'은 동사가 명사, 형용사, 부사로 성격전환한다.

일반적으로 '동사'는 주어 뒤에서 '주어의 동사'에서만 사용될 수 있다. 그래서 주어의 동사자리가 아닌 곳에서는 동사가 사용 될 수 없다. 다만 동사의 성격을 바꿔 주면 다른 곳에서 사용될 수 있다.

그 동사의 성격을 바꿔 줄 수 있는 방법 중 하나가 'to 동사원형'이다. 앞에서 배운 '동사원형ing'등도 있다.

'to 동사원형'은 명사, 형용사, 부사로 사용될 수 있다. 즉 명사의 자리인 주어, 목적어, 주어보충어 자리에 사용될 수 있다. 또 형용사가 사용될 수 있는 명사 뒤와 보충어(주어보충어와 목적어 보충어)자리에서 사용될 수도 있다. 또한 부사처럼 문장전체를 꾸며주거나 형용사나 부사를 꾸며 줄 수도 있다.

명사용법	형용사용법	부사용법	
주어, 목적어, 주어보충어 자리에서 사용	명사 뒤, 주어보충어, 목적어보충어자리에서 사용	문장전체 수식	형용사나 부사수식
~하는 것	~ 할	감정의 원인, 목적, 결과, 이유, 조건	

Study **01** 명사용법 (~하는 것)

1. 주어

- **To ride** a bike is fun.   자전거를 타는 것을 재미있다.
- **To swim** in the sea is dangerous.   바다에서 수영하는 것은 위험하다.

다만 주어자리는 간단하게 쓰고자 하는 영어문장의 원리 때문에 허수아비인 가짜주어 it를 쓰고 진짜 주어를 뒤로 뺄 수 있다. 즉 위의 문장은 다음과 같이 각각 쓸 수 있다.

- **To ride** a bike is fun.   자전거를 타는 것은 재미있다.
  - → It is fun **to ride** a bike.

- **To swim** in the sea is dangerous.   바다에서 수영하는 것은 위험하다.
  - → It is dangerous **to swim** in the sea .

다음 문장을 'to 동사원형'에 유념하여 해석하시오.

(01). <u>To ride</u> a bike is easy.

→ It is easy <u>to ride</u> a bike.

→ _____

(02). <u>To exercise</u> regularly is necessary.

→ It is necessary <u>to exercise</u> regularly.

→ _____

(03). <u>To read</u> a lot of books is important.

→ It is important <u>to read</u> a lot of books.

→ _____

(04). <u>To go</u> to a concert is exciting.

→ It is exciting <u>to go</u> to a concert.

→ _____

(05). <u>To recycle</u> the bottles is important.

→ It is important <u>to recycle</u> the bottles.

→ _____

(06). <u>To spend</u> so much time playing computer games is not good.

→It is not good <u>to spend</u> so much time playing computer games.

→ _____

2. 목적어

- She hopes **to be** a doctor someday.
- Tony loves **to make** machines.

그녀는 언젠가 의사가 되는 것을 원한다.

Tony는 기계를 만드는 것을 좋아한다.

 확인문제 2

다음 문장을 'to 동사원형'에 유념하여 해석하시오.

(01). Would you like **to join** our activity?

→ _____

(02. John hopes **to become** a baseball player.

→ _____

(03). We expect **to do** better next time.

→ _____

(04). Salley wants **to visit** Europe during summer break time.

→ _____

(05). Jack wants **to spend** my money wisely.

→ _____

(06). Mom decided not **to go** out because of the weather.

→ _____

(07). It's a nice day, so I want **to go** for a walk.

→ _____

(08). We plan **to visit** our grandparents tomorrow.

→ _____

(09). A lot of people want **to become** marathoners.

→ _____

(10). Some people always want **to run** in tougher conditions.

→ _____

《정답과 해설 19P》

further study

목적어자리에서 'to 동사원형'과 '동사원형ing'

A. 목적어 자리에 동사가 왔을 때, 나중일을 나타내는 want 등 미래성 동사는 'to 동사원형', enjoy 등 항상 그렇다는 항시성 동사는 '동사원형ing'가 온다.

⊙ 'to 동사원형'을 목적어로 취하는 미래성 동사: want, hope, wish, expect, decide, plan
  • We want to ioin the club.   우리는 그 클럽에 참여하는 것을 원한다.

⊙ '동사원형ing'를 목적어로 취하는 항시성동사: enjoy, finish, give up, avoid, mind
  • My dad enjoys playing baseball.   나의 아빠는 야구를 하는 것을 즐긴다.

B. like나 love등 뜻 차이 없이 'to 동사원형'과 '동사원형ing' 둘 다 오는 동사들도 있다.

⊙ 뜻 차이 없이 'to 동사원형'과 '동사원형ing'를 모두 목적어로 취하는 동사: like, love, start, begin, continue
  • The children like to swim here.
    = The children like swimming here.   그 아이들은 여기에서 수영하는 것을 좋아한다.

C. 뜻이 달라지는 동사

⊙ 나중일을 나타낼 때는 'to 동사원형'을, 과거일을 나타낼 때는 '동사원형ing'가 오는 동사: remember, forget
  • 나중일: I remember to give her the books.   나는 그녀에게 책을 줄 것을 기억하고 있다.
    과거일: I remember giving her the books.   나는 그녀에게 책을 주었던 것을 기억하고 있다.

 확인문제 3

다음 문장에서 어법상 맞지 않는 것을 찾아 올바로 고치시오. 그리고 해석하시오.

(01). He decided to go to the party.

(02). The writer finished to write a novel.

(03) They planned helping the handicapped.

(04). The Coast Guide avoided to search for the lost ship.

(05). The boy remembered mailing the letter tomorrow.

(06). She forgot to meet her friends then.

(07). The children enjoy to play baseball.

(08). The girls like chatting with their friends.

(09). Customers hope buying cheaper goods.

(10). The dog likes run with his owner.

《정답과 해설 20P》

3. 보충어: ~하는 것

• My hope is <u>to collect</u> coins.　　　　　　나의 희망은 동전을 모으는 것이다.

 확인문제 4

다음 문장을 'to 동사원형'에 유념하여 해석하시오.

(01). Their object is <u>to get</u> a good job.

　　→ _____

(02). My plan is <u>to travel</u> to Africa this summer.

　　→ _____

(03). His next impulse is <u>to look</u> at Bree for help.

　　→ _____

(04). My hope is <u>to major</u> in boilogy.

　　→ _____

《정답과 해설 20P》

Study 02 형용사용법

1. 명사 뒤: ～할

- I have a lot of work <u>to do</u>.
- Students have homework <u>to do</u>.
- He set aside time <u>to read</u>.
- There were no malls <u>to hang</u> out at.
- Pollution is also a factor <u>to consider</u>.

나는 해야 할 많은 일을 가지고 있다.
학생들은 해야할 숙제를 가지고 있다.
그는 읽을 시간을 떼어 놓았다.
놀만한 몰들이 없었다.
오염은 또한 고려할 요소이다.

2. 주어보충어: ～할 예정, 가능성

- The player is <u>to join</u> the team.
- The examinees are <u>to pass</u> the entrance exam.

그 선수는 그 팀에 합류할 예정이다.
그 수험생들은 입학 시험에 합격할 수 있다.

3. 목적어보충어

- My parents want me <u>to major</u> in medicine.
- The villagers allowed the old man <u>to stay</u> there.

나의 부모님은 내가 의학을 전공하기를 원한다.

그 마을 사람들은 그 노인이 거기에 머무르라고 허락했다.

 확인문제 5

다음 문장에서 밑줄 친 'to 동사원형'이 어떤 명사를 꾸며주는가를 유념하여 해석하시오.

(01). It's time **to get** up.

→ _____

(02). Sally has nothing **to worry** about.

→ _____

(03). I made a plan **to go** shopping with her.

→ _____

(04). Jessica wanted to buy a couch **to sit on**.

→ _____

(05). Minho has lots of things **to do** tonight.

→ _____

(06). There are many places **to visit** in Korea.

→ _____

(07). We had no chance **to talk** together.

→ _____

(08). We need to buy something **to eat**.

→ _____

(09). My father didn't find a shirt **to wear**.

→ _____

(10). Gyeongju was a nice city **to visit**.

→ _____

《정답과 해설 20P》

Study 03 부사용법

1. 문장전체 수식

① 감정의 원인

- I'm happy **to hear** that.   나는 그것을 들으니 행복하다.
- We are pleased **to meet** an entertainer.   우리는 연예인을 만나서 기쁘다.

② 목적

- She studies **to be** a music teacher.   그녀는 음악 선생님이 되기 위해서 공부한다.
- I took a taxi **to arrive** there in time.   나는 거기에 제 시간에 도착하기 위해서 택시를 탔다.

③ 결과

- He woke up **to find** the whole house on fire.   그는 깨어서 전체 집이 불에 타고 있는 것을 발견했다.

④ 이유

- The man must be a single **to seem** lonely.   그 남자는 외롭게 보이니 싱글임에 틀림없다.

⑤ 조건

- **To pass** the exam, you must study hard.   시험에 합격하고자 한다면 너는 열심히 공부해야한다.

2. 형용사나 부사 수식

- Philo was ready **to find** new investors.   필로는 새로운 투자자를 찾을 준비가 되어 있었다.
- A computer is able **to access** information from sensors in the car.
                                                               컴퓨터는 차에 있는 센서로부터 정보에 접근할 수 있다.

 확인문제 6

다음 문장에 쓰인 'to 동사원형'은 부사적 용법이다. 각각 '감정의 원인', '목적', '결과', '이유', '조건' 중 무엇이 해당되는 지를 말하고 해석하시오.

(01). I'm happy <u>to help</u> you.

→ _____

(02). She went abroad <u>to study</u> English.

→ _____

(03). I went to the store <u>to buy</u> a jacket.

→ _____

(04). Sam went to the airport <u>to pick</u> her up.

→ _____

(05). I stopped <u>to listen</u> to music.

→ _____

(06). Jack must be sick <u>to seem</u> pale.

→ _____

(07). The doctors are happy <u>to find</u> a new cure.

→ _____

(08). I used my smart phone <u>to do</u> my homework.

→ _____

(09). He grew up <u>to be</u> a famous painter.

→ _____

(10). <u>To be</u> a good runner, you must exercise everyday.

<안내> 《정답과 해설 20P》

Grammar in Reading

《정답과 해설 20~20》

1. 아래 글에서 어법상 맞지 않는 부분을 찾아 올바로 고치시오.

English speakers say 'thank you' very often speak politely. Also they often use 'please' as another way. When they want be polite, they say 'would you', 'could you' or 'would you like to'.

2. 아래 글에서 어법상 맞지 않는 부분을 찾아 올바로 고치시오.

My name is Wonky. I'm 13 years old and I'll be 14 on May 17th. I was born and still to live in Texas, U. S. A. I'd like make friends from other countries. I enjoy play basketball and swimming. I want be a basketball player. Please e-mail me; scy7469@hanmail.com.

3. 아래 글의 밑줄 친 (A)와 (B)와 각각 같은 용법인 것을 모두 고르시오.

M: I heard your friend went to Vietnam last month.

W: Yeah, he went there (A) <u>to do</u> volunteer work in a Vietnamese village.

M: Really? What did he do?

W: He painted the school walls and fixed desks and chairs.

M: Wow, sounds great!

W: Yeah. I hope (B) <u>to go</u> abroad to help others.

M: I'm sure you will someday.

①. Bora decides <u>to do</u> the science homework first.

②. She wants <u>to take</u> a test again.

③. He was looking for a chair <u>to sit</u> on.

④. It is impossible <u>to meet</u> the dead line.

⑤. They were in hurry <u>to finish</u> their project on time.

⑥. Roosevelt worked <u>to protect</u> the wildlife.

⑦. I went to the market <u>to buy</u> some fruit.

⑧. He grew a mustache <u>to look</u> older.

⑨. The boy has nothing <u>to speak</u> about.

⑩. We went to the station <u>to see</u> him off..

01.(A)-   02. (B)-

Grammar in Reading

《정답과 해설 21P》

4. 아래 글의 밑줄 친 (A), (B)와 같은 용법인 것을 모두 고르시오.

M: Do you have any plans for this Saturday?

W: No, not really.

M: Then, do you want (A)<u>to go</u> to watch a baseball game with me? I have two tickets.

W: Sure. Which teams are playing?

M: The Dragons and the Unicorns.

W: What time does the game start?

M: It starts at two, but I'm planning (B)<u>to get</u> to the ballpark by one.

W: Okay, I'll meet you there at one.

①. You need <u>to learn</u> English.

②. We're happy <u>to come</u> to Korea.

③. He was looking for the chair <u>to sit</u> on.

④. They have some pictures <u>to show</u> you.

⑤. We call the hotel desk <u>to ask</u> for an extra pillow.

⑥. She needs somebody <u>to push</u> her wheelchair.

⑦. Junsu wished <u>to be</u> good at speaking English like Suji.

⑧. Junsu likes <u>to communicate</u> with a foreigner in English.

⑨. The manager went to the post office <u>to send</u> a letter to her.

⑩. The movie is not good <u>to watch</u> with children.

1. 다음 문장에서 각각 틀린 문장을 찾아 올바로 고치시오. 그리고 해석하세요.

01. To see is believe.

→ _____

02. He doesn't have anything drink.

→ _____

03. He will go abroad study more.

→ _____

04. Mina's future dream is be a nurse.

→ _____

05. I ran to school early not be late for school.

→ _____

06. I need a book read.

→ _____

07. I like listen to music.

→ _____

08. I will go there see him.

→ _____

09. I want see a movie tonight.

→ _____

10. Learn English is not very difficult.

→ _____

11. Semin loves play computer games.

→ _____

12. Jim wanted borrow that pen from you.

→ _____

13. They didn't have any books read.

→ _____

14. Michael bought a dog be less lonely.

→ _____

15. Junho practiced really hard be a good dancer.

→ _____

16. We moved forward see the singer nearby.

→ _____

17. Philo set out fix the machine himself.

→ _____

18. Finally, the school band showed up and started play.

→ _____

19. You should go to bed early catch the first bus tomorrow.

→ _____

20. Sally went to the park play badminton.

→ _____

2. 다음 각각의 문장에서 사용된 'to+동사원형'이 명사용법인지, 형용사용법인지, 부사용법인지를 말하고 각각 해석하시오.

01. He studied hard **to become** a doctor.

→ _____, _____

02. Mike bought a gift **to give** his sister.

→ _____, _____

03. My younger sister didn't have anything **to do**.

→ _____, _____

04. Chris runs everyday **to become** healthy.

　→ _____, _____

05. Sally went to the park **to meet** her friend.

　→ _____, _____

06. She learns English **to make** foreign friends.

　→ _____, _____

07. The old man lived **to be** 100 years old.

　→ _____, _____

08. I don't want **to eat** these vegetables anymore.

　→ _____, _____

09. John hopes **to become** a baseball player.

　→ _____, _____

10. We have found ways **to help** them.

　→ _____, _____

11. I hope **to give** medical help to the people in poor countries.

　→ _____, _____

12. I met Peter **to give** him the information.

　→ _____, _____

3. 다음 밑줄 친 부분의 'to 동사원형'의 쓰임이 다른 것은?

01.

①. He has no house **to live** in.

②. I have a lot of homework **to do**.

③. We went to the station **to see** him off.

《정답과 해설 00p》

④. Would you like something **to drink**?

⑤. Do you want a magazine **to read**?.

02.
①. **To swim** in the sea is dangerous.

②. She wants **to buy** a big house.

③. He has a hat **to wear** in the sun.

④. I want **to have** lunch with you.

⑤. We expect **to do** better next time.

03.
①. I turned on the computer **to play** games.

②. She is going to the post office **to send** a letter.

③. Hana went to the library **to study** for the final exam.

④. Tony opened the door **to watch** the birds in the tree.

⑤. Her purpose in life is **to become** a famous pianist.

04.
①. We went to his house **to fix** the computer.

②. We need to buy something **to eat**.

③. My father didn't find a shirt **to wear**.

④. I have some questions **to ask** you.

⑤. Do you have enough time **to help** me?

05.
① There was not any chair **to sit** on.

② He put his hand on his hat **to say** hello to me.

③ Mina went to library **to read** some books.

④ You'd better wear sunglasses **to protect** your eyes.

⑤ Ann visited the professor's office **to ask** about the test.

06.
① I have some pictures **to show** you.

② He has a lot of work **to do**.

③ I have no money **to give** him

④ The hotel is a convenient place **to stay**.

⑤ Scott needs a new camera **to take** nice pictures.

4. 아래 보기의 문장에서 쓰인 'to 동사원형'이 밑줄 친 부분의 'to 동사원형'의 쓰임과 같은 것은?(2개 인 경우도 있음)

01.
보기: He got a chance **to answer**

①. She kept the promise **to come** back home early.

②. He must be a fool **to believe** such a thing.

③. Few people live **to be** a hundred years old.

④. He is quick **to see** the faults of others.

⑤. They contracted with my father **to do** the work.

02.
　　보기: My grandmother needs a chair **to sit** on.

①. He worked hard **to succeed**.

②. There is no friend **to depend** on.

③. She grew up **to be** a doctor.

④. I am happy **to meet** you.

⑤. He left his home, never **to return** again.

03.
　　보기: Lisa likes **to get** up early in the morning.

①. She promised not **to be** late for school.

②. She grew up **to be** a famous singer.

③. I studied hard **to pass** the exam.

④. I forgot **to send** a letter to my mother.

⑤. I could not find a place **to stay**.

04.
　　보기: She borrowed some books **to read** on her journey.

①. The purpose of industry is **to create** wealth.

②. Monkeys use a stick **to catch** their prey.

③. They didn't have books for children **to read**.

④. <u>To have</u> a brother is to have a lifetime friend.

⑤. She decided <u>to get</u> into movies when young.

05.
보기: I got up early <u>to get</u> ready for the game.

①. Sally went to the park <u>to play</u> badminton.

②. The children went <u>to see</u> a baseball game.

③. They want <u>to meet</u> you again.

④. I want the pencil <u>to write</u> with.

⑤. <u>To do</u> that work is very difficult.

Chapter

06

Uses of Past Paticiple
과거분사 사용

p.p-과거분사의 사용

일반적으로 동사는 주어 뒤에서 주어의 동사로만 사용 된다. 하지만 주어의 동사가 아닌 곳에서는 동사의 성격을 바꿔 주어야 한다. 동사의 3단 변화형 중 3번째인 'p.p-과거분사'는 외부적인 힘에 의해 이루어지는 '수동'적인 의미를 나타낸다.

동사의 성격을 바꿔 줄 수 있는, 앞에서 배운 '동사원형ing'와 'to 동사원형'과 함께 3가지 성격전환 방법 중 한가지이다.

'p.p-과거분사'는 형용사처럼 명사의 앞이나 뒤, 주어 보충어, 목적어 보충어자리에서 명사를 꾸며주기 위하여 사용된다. 또 원인, 조건, 시간, 동시동작, 연속동작, 상황상관없음을 나타내며 부사처럼 문장전체를 꾸며준다.

형용사용법		부사용법	
- 명사 앞 - 명사 뒤 - 주어 보충어 - 목적어 보충어	~ 되어진(수동적)	– 원인	~ 때문에
		– 조건	~ 한다면
		– 시간	~할 때, ~한 후에 ~하는 동안에
		– 동시동작	~ 하면서
		– 연속동작	그리고 ~하다
		–상황상관없음	~ 일 지라도

Study 01 수동적 의미의 형용사

형용사처럼 명사앞, 명사뒤, 주어보충어, 목적어보충어 자리에서 명사를 꾸며준다.

① 명사 앞

- Why do you try our **roasted** chicken?   너는 왜 우리의 구운 닭을 먹느냐?
- The **fermented** food, "Yogurt" is good for health.   발효음식 요구르트는 건강을 위하여 좋다.

② 명사 뒤

- Our ancestors loved rice cakes **made** with flowers.   우리 조상들은 꽃으로 만들어진 떡을 좋아했다.
- The answer is "kimchi", **thought** of as the national dish of Korea.

  정답은 한국의 국민음식이라고 생각되어진 김치이다.

③ 주어보충어

- **Yogurt** is **produced**.   요구르트가 생산되어진다.
- **Milk** is **fermented** by certain bacteria.   우유는 어떤 박테리아에 의해서 발효된다.

④ 목적어 보충어

- He had his hair **cut** short.   그는 머리를 짧게 깎았다.
- The girl had her picture **taken**.   그 소녀는 자신의 사진을 찍게 했다.

 확인문제 1

다음 밑줄 그은 'p.p-과거분사'가 꾸며주는 명사를 쓰시오. (형용사로 쓰이는 'p.p-과거분사'는
앞이나 뒤의 (대)명사, 또는 주어나 목적어에 있는 (대)명사를 꾸며준다.)

(01). The door was <u>repaired</u>.

(02). This is a <u>sold</u> house by my dad.

(03). It is no use over <u>spilt</u> milk.

(04). Repair the <u>broken</u> window.

(05). The manager had the computer <u>fixed</u>.

(06). Do you meet a man <u>injured</u> at the accident?

《정답과 해설 23P》

다음 괄호 안의 단어를 알맞은 형태로 바꾸어 빈칸에 쓰시오.

(01). The _____ car is very good. (fix)

(02). Now do you have a _____ room? (clean)

(03). A box _____ by an old man is very heavy. (carry)

(04). The passengers had their picture _____. (take)

(05). This newspaper is _____ by many people. (read)

(06). The picture was _____ yesterday. (steal)

(07). We saw the car _____ on the road. (carry)

(08). The manager had the goods _____ in the garage. (pile)

(09). That song was _____ by David Smith in 1995. (sing)

(10). The chair was _____ by my younger brother. (break)

(11). The elephants were _____ by the people. (catch)

(12). The room is _____ by Susie. (clean)

(13). The hospital was _____ by us. (build)

(14). The kids saw the robot _____ by a controller. (move)

(15). These toys are _____ by Mr. Han. (make)

further study 부사용법

부사절 중에서 원인, 조건, 시간, 동시동작, 연속동작, 상황상관없음에 해당하는 부사절이 간단히 된 것이다. 원래는 '동사원형ing'가 온다. be동사인 경우는 'Being'이지만 'Being'이 생략되어 'p.p-과거분사'가 된 것이다.

1. 원인- as, because 등

- (Being) Known to many people, his novel sells well.

  (← As his novel is known to many people, it sells well.)

  많은 사람들에게 알려졌기 때문에 그의 소설은 잘 팔린다.

2. 조건- if

- (Being) Fixed, this computer will be good enough to use.

  (← If this computer is fixed, it will be good enough to use.)

  이 컴퓨터가 수리되면 사용에기에 충분할 것이다.

3. 시간- as, when, after 등

- (Being) Carried to the airport, the baggage was loaded into the plane.

  (← After the baggage was carried to the airport, it was loaded into the plane.)

  그 수화물이 공항에 옮겨진 후 비행기에 실렸다.

4. 동시동작 - as

- (Being) Burned, the factory was exploded.)

  (← As the factory was burned, it was exploded.)

  그 공장이 불에 타면서 폭발했다.

5. 연속동작 - and

• Nelson Mandela fought for justice, (being) elected president.

(← He fought for justice, and he was elected president.)

넬슨 만델라는 정의를 위하여 싸웠다. 그리고 대통령으로 선출되었다.

6. 상황상관없음- though, although

• (Being) Surprised at the incident, president remained silent.

(← Though he was surprised at the incident, president remained silent.)

대통령은 그 사고에 놀랐지만 침묵한 상태로 남아 있었다.

 확인문제 3

다음문장에서 밑줄 친 'p.p-과거분사'가 원인, 조건, 시간, 동시동작, 연속동작, 상황상관없음 중 무엇으로 사용되었는지를 말하고 각각 해석하시오.

(01). Cleaned by mom, my room was clean.

(02). Informed of the good news, he was happy.

(03). Praised, children will study hard.

(04). The tree grew tall, cut by a neighbor.

(05). Watched by the police, the people marched along the street.

(06). Helped by many people, he failed in the business.

《정답과 해설 23P》

Study 02 구간시제(완료시제)에서 p.p-과거분사

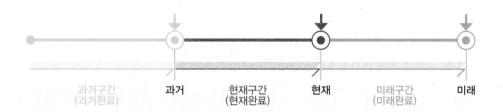

구간시제는 한 시점이 아니고 일정구간을 나타내는 시제이다. 즉 과거에서 현재까지의 구간을 나타내는 시제는 <u>현재구간(현재완료)</u>, 앞선과거에서 과거까지의 구간을 나타내는 시제는 <u>과거구간(과거완료)</u>, 미래까지를 나타내는 시제를 <u>미래구간(미래완료)</u>이라고 한다.

① 현재구간- 'have/has p.p' 형태: 과거와 현재를 동시에 표현하는 표현법이다.
- The fox **has met** ducklings.　　　　　　　여우가 오리새끼들을 만났다.
- Pigs **have** ever **seen** a tiger.　　　　　돼지들이 지금까지 호랑이를 본적이 있다.
- The giraffe **has** ever **seen** a lion.　　　기린이 지금까지 사자를 본적이 있다.
- You **have** never **seen** any ducklings.　너는 지금까지 어떠한 오리새끼들도 본적이 없다.

cf) 명백한 과거를 나타내는 yesterday, last year 등은 과거부터 현재까지를 나타내는 현재구간과는 함께 쓸 수 없다. 반드시 과거동사를 써야 한다.
- Eunice went to her hometown village yesterday.　Eunice는 어제 그녀의 고향 마을에 갔다.

② 과거구간- 'had+p.p'
- By the time he retired, Pele **had scored** 1,281 goals.　펠레가 은퇴할 때까지 1,281골을 득점했다.
- He **had scored** more goals than any other soccer player at that time.
　　　　　　　　　　　　　　　　　　　　　　그는 그 당시 어떠한 선수보다도 더 많은 득점을 했다.

③ 미래구간 -'will have p.p'
- Winter **will have come** next month.　　　겨울은 다음 달에 올 것이다.
- The swallows **will have come** here by next week.　제비가 다음 주 쯤 까지 이곳에 올 것이다.

아래 각각 문장에서 _____ 에 알맞은 형태의 동사를 쓰시오.

(01). Have you ever _____ of this actor? (hear)

(02). Have you ever _____ Korea, Cathy? (visit)

(03). Have you _____ all of the six kids? (see)

(04). My son has never _____ a pizza. (eat)

(05). No one has _____ his record yet. (break)

(06). Your contribution has _____ so much.(help)

(07). My family have ever _____ to the zoo.(be)

(08). A monkey has often _____ a tree.(climb)

(09). Jane, have you ever _____ a presentation in class?(make)

(10). I haven't even _____ , and I have only two days left.(start)

Grammar in Reading

《정답과 해설 241》

1. 다음 (　　　) 안에 주어진 동사의 알맞은 단어의 형태를 쓰시오.

Have you ⓐ (hear) of Cupid, the god of love? Maybe you have ⓑ (see) his image around Valentine's Day. He looks like a young boy with a small bow and arrows. But his bow and arrows are very powerful and can make people fall in and out of love. Apollo was the god of the Sun. He was a great hunter. Cupid respected Apollo very much and wanted to be like him. However, Apollo just thought of Cupid as a weak little boy. One day, Apollo saw Cupid playing and said, "Stop playing with your little bow and arrows. You will never be a real hunter like me."

01. ⓐ-   02. ⓑ-

2. 다음 글에서 (　　　) 안에 주어진 단어의 알맞은 형태를 쓰시오.

The earth is a ⓐ (close) system. Only energy from the sun enters, and only heat energy from the earth is ⓑ (remove). Everything else on the earth is ⓒ (reuse). Water to drink is the same water that was here millions of years ago. It is used, ⓓ (clean) up, and used again. When you drink water, you may be using some water that was once ⓔ (drink) by George Washington, or a dinosaur, and maybe even yourself a long time ago.

01. ⓐ-   02. ⓑ-   03. ⓒ-
04. ⓓ-   05. ⓔ-

(정답과 해설 24P)

1. 다음 (   ) 안의 동사를 p.p(과거분사)로 쓰시오.

01. "Blue jeans" were (   ) here.(bear)

02. I am very (   ) to hear that.(please)

03. The poems are (   ) in English.(write)

04. The man was (   ) president.(elect)

05. Blacks were (   ) from Africa.(bring)

06. A new machine was (   ) in 1865.(invent)

07. The most money was (   ) by miners.(make)

08. My life was (   ) into the unknown.(throw)

09. Your seats have been (   ) successfully.(reserve)

10. The Korean flag is (   ) the Taegeukgi.(call)

11. Abraham Lincoln was (   ) president.(elect)

12. Blacks from Africa were (   ) as slaves.(use)

13. Lincoln was (   ) president in 1864. (reelect)

14. Washington was (   ) leader of the army. (name)

15. The valley is also (   ) as Silicon Valley.(know)

16. The notice was (   ) high in the bulletin board.(write)

17. This kingdom is (   ) with wonderful creatures. (fill)

18. The child was (   ) when he saw a goat.(frighten)

19. The machine was (   ) of wood and metal tires.(make)

20. People became (   ) in their physical fitness.(interest)

2. 다음 (   ) 안의 문장에 p.p(과거분사)를 쓰시오.

01. The gears of their ten-speed bikes are never (   ).(use)

02. The machine became (   ) as the hobby horse.(know)

03. The son of a rich planter was (   ) to be a surveyor. (educate)

04. The old woman was deeply (   ) by what he said.(move)

05. The bridge was (   ) in 1869 by an old man. (suggest)

06. The machine was (   ) in a park or a garden as a toy.(enjoy)

07. The machine was (   ) by pushing your feet against the ground.(move)

08. George Washington was (   ) in military leader-ship. (interest)

09. Kim Dae-Jung is commonly (   ) the first president of democracy in Korea.(call)

10. The big island of Hawaii is (   ) with lava rocks and live volcanoes.(cover)

3. 다음 각각의 문장에 (   ) 안에 알맞은 단어의 형태를 쓰시오..

01. Namul is a kind of (   ) vegetable. (boil)

02. These are cookies (   ) by the chef. (make)

03. I met a famous scientist (   ) Newton. (name)

04. Do you know a man (   ) Mechnikov? (call)

05. The smell of popcorn (   ) the air. (fill)

06. There is a house (   ) with dogs on the hill. (fill)

07. Many businesses (   ) the Special Olympics.(sponsor)

08. Did you have the books (   ) to the library? (return)

09. They raised $58,000, the amount (   ) to purchase the ad. (need)

10. The people in the world watched Sewol ferry (   ) in TV.(sink)

4. 다음 각각 문장에서 틀린 것이 있는 문장을 찾아 고치시오.

01. Those cookies were make by my mom

_____ → _____

02. A lot of books are read by Dad.

_____ → _____

03. I am inviting to the party every year by Jason.

_____ → _____ _____

04. This building was built by in the 17th century.

_____ → _____

05. Jane was introduced to them by her friend.

_____ → _____

06. Nine symphonies composed by Beethoven in his life.

_____ → _____

07. *Star Wars* was directed by George Lucas.

_____ → _____

08. Some bread was bought by the manager.

_____ → _____

09. The letters were readed by him yesterday.

_____ → _____

10. This machine was invent by my father.

_____ → _____

11. French can spoken and written by my friend.

_____ → _____

12. His promise will broken by Jimin.

_____ → _____

13. The problem must solve by him.

_____ → _____

14. Mrs. Dorothy was bought some bread.

_____ → _____

15. This book is read many students.

_____ → _____

16. Some books are bought by Dad last night.

_____ → _____

17. This car were made in Korea.

_____ → _____

18. Only two votes were elected Amy captain of our team

_____ → _____

5. 아래 각각 문장에서 _____ 에 알맞은 형태의 동사를 쓰시오.

01. She has _____ (go).

02. How much have you _____ so far?(prepare)

03. The squirrels have ever _____ acorns. (eat)

04. The snake has ever _____ a strawberry.(eat)

05. The elephants have never _____ a dinosaur.(see)

06. The baby has ever _____ off the bed.(fall)

07. Have you ever _____ poems in English? (read)

08. You have _____ me to write a piece on animals.(ask)

09. I have never _____ in any other political office. (serve)

10. The kittens have ever _____ to sleep in Mommy and Daddy's bed. (want)

6. 다음 문장을 해석하시오.

01. He has not written the report yet.
   → _____

02. They have been at the camp for three days.
   → _____

03. Minho has taken pictures of the palace.
   → _____

04. The writer has borrowed some books about the palace.
   → _____

05. The cartoonist has found information on the Internet.
→ _____

06. The bride has been in her room for one hour.
→ _____

07. The bridegroom has just sent e-mails to his friends.
→ _____

08. She has not bought the cake and flowers yet.
→ _____

09. The criminal has not eaten anything all day.
→ _____

10. How long have the students been at the camp?
→ _____

11. Jack and Paul have just finished dinner.
→ _____

12. You have already sent this person a friend request.
→ _____

7. 다음 각각의 문장에서 어법상 틀린 문장을 찾아 올바로 쓰시오.

01. I have never readed an English novel.
→ _____

02. She has met her husband in Paris last year.
→ _____

03. I have never seen such clear sea water.
→ _____

04. Have you ever hear of the Golden Gate Bridge?
→ _____

05. I have visited some famous places in Seoul 5 days ago.
→ _____

06. It rains for three days.
→ _____

07. James has gone to Tokyo last year.
→ _____

08. I have gone to New York twice.
→ _____

09. We have known each other for we were young.
→ _____

10. My sister lost a bag.(= She doesn't have it now)
→ _____

11. A: Have you seen Mary lately? B: Yes, I have. I have seen her at school yesterday.
→ _____

12. The pants, "blue jeans", were not making for young people, but for miners.
→ _____

8. 다음 각 문제에서 제시된 두 개의 문장을 괄호 안에 주어진 단어를 이용하여 한 문장으로 표현하시오.

01. I started to work here a month ago. I still work here.
→ _____ (for)

02. The manager started to work at the cafe in 2001. He still works there.
→ _____ (since)

03. Jack arrived here four days ago. He's here now.

→ _____ (be/for)

04. Yujin began to study English 8 years ago. She still studies it.

→ _____(for)

05. My mom bought the house last year. She still has it.

→ _____ (own/since)

06. Dad bought this car 10 years ago. Dad drives this car now.

→ _____ (drive/for)

07. Anderson started to learn Korean in 2003. He learns Korean now.

→ _____ (since)

08. My sister was in her room two hours ago. She is there now.

→ _____ (for)

09. I lost my wallet, so I don't have it now.

→ _____

10. My sister lost her watch, but she doesn't have it now.

→ _____

9. 다음을 (   ) 안의 어휘를 사용하여 영작하시오.

01. 나는 2005년 이후 피아노를 쳐왔다.(since)

→ _____

02. 그는 런던에 가 본 적이 없다.(not/be)

→ _____

03. Anderson은 한국어를 5년 동안 배우고 있다.(learn/for)

→ _____

정답과 해설 267

04. 나는 Lucas씨를 만난 적이 없다.(never/meet)

　→ _____

05. 너는 전에 영문 소설을 읽어 본 적이 있니?(ever/before)

　→ _____?

06. 너는 폴란드에 가 본 적이 있니? (ever/Poland/before)

　→ _____?

07. 나는 어릴 적 이후로 영화를 본 적이 없다.(never/since)

　→ _____

08. 그의 누이는 그를 만난 적이 없습니다.(never/before)

　→ _____

09. 나의 아빠는 홍콩에 가 본 적이 있다. (be)

　→ _____

10. 그녀의 여동생은 호랑이를 본적이 없다. (not)

　→ _____

11. 너는 중국에 가본 적이 있느냐?(ever/be)

　→ _____

12. 나의 아들은 이전에 고래를 본적이 결코 없다. (never/before)

　→ _____

13. 그는 지금 막 숙제를 끝냈다.(just/finish/his)

　→ _____

14. Jane은 한국에 가고 없다.(go/Korea/to)

　→ _____

15. 너는 지금까지 Santa Clara Valley에 대해 들어본 적이 있어요?(ever/heard)

　→ _____

Chapter

07

Auxiliary Verbs
조동사

조동사는 동사를 돕는 역할을 한다. 일반적으로 조동사 다음에 동사원형이 온다. 다만 may, must, can't, should 다음에 'have+p.p'가 와서 과거와 관련된 내용을 표현한다.

Study 01 do

3인칭 단수	does	과거형	did	과거분사형	done
부정문		의문문		동사 강조	

1. 부정문

• We **don't** go to church.   우리는 교회에 가지 않는다.
• Mom **doesn't** cook at home.   엄마는 집에서 요리하지 않는다.

2. 의문문

• **Do** you have any magazines to read?   읽을 잡지 있어요?
• What **does** he teach at school?   그가 학교에서 무엇을 가르치나요?

3. 동사강조

• He **does** prepare our family's lunch.   그는 우리 가족의 점심을 준비한다.
• The detective **did** detect the lost car.   그 탐정은 잃어버린 차를 찾았다.
• We **do** exchange our present at Christmas.   우리는 크리스마스에 우리의 선물을 교환한다.

cf) do는 조동사가 아닌 일반동사로도 사용된다.
• The students do their homework in the evening.   그 학생들은 저녁에 그들의 숙제를 한다.

확인문제 1

다음 문장을 부정문으로 고치시오.

(01). You look very slim.

→ _____

(02). Mom takes your trash back home.

→ _____

(03). Lucy learned tennis.

→ _____

《정답과 해설 26P》

확인문제 2

다음 문장을 의문문으로 고치시오.

(01). You cross the streets.

→ _____

(02). She waits for the green light.

→ _____

(03). The cyclist wore a helmet.

→ _____

《정답과 해설 26P》

확인문제 3

다음 문장에서 동사를 강조하시오.

(01). You borrow my cell phone.

→ _____

(02). James comes to my birthday party.

→ _____

(03). They parked their cars here.

→ _____

(04). We use his room and office.

→ _____

《정답과 해설 26P》

Study 02 will

미래를 나타낸다. will은 'be(am, are, is) going to 동사원형'으로 바꿔 쓸 수 있다.

- He **will** go abroad. (=He <u>is going to</u> go abroad.)   그는 외국에 갈 것이다.
- The book **will** help you study English. (=The book <u>is going to</u> help you study English.)

  그 책은 네가 영어를 공부하는데 도와줄 것이다.

 확인문제 4

다음 문장을 be going to를 이용하여 다시 쓰시오.

(01). He will go home now.

→ _____

(02). We will go to bed early.

→ _____

(03). I will do my homework.

→ _____

(04). They will get up early.

→ _____

(05). You will use a cell phone.

→ _____

(06). We will arrive at the station at noon.

→ _____

《정답과 해설 26p》

Study 03 may

허가 (=can)	추측(가능성) →It is possible that 주어+동사 ～
～ 해도 좋다.	～일지도 모른다.

1. 허가: ～해도 좋다

- You **may** borrow my cell phone.
- You **may** park your car here.
- **May** I have a glass of water, please?

너는 나의 휴대폰을 빌려도 좋아.
너는 여기에 너의 차를 주차해도 돼.
물 한 잔 주시겠어요?

2. 추측(가능성): ～일지도 모른다

현재나 미래 추측	may 동사원형 ～(→It is possible that 주어+현재동사)
과거추측	may have p.p ～ (→ It is possible that 주어+과거동사)

(1). 현재나 미래 추측: **may 동사원형 ～(→It is possible that 주어+현재동사/will 동사원형); ～일지도 모른다.**

- She **may** have money.
  (→It is possible that she has money.)

그녀는 돈을 가지고 있을지 몰라.

- James **may** come to my birthday party.
  (→It is possible that James will come to my birthday party.)

제임스는 나의 생일파티에 올 수 있어.

(2). 과거추측: may have p.p ~ (→It is possible that 주어+과거동사); ~이었을지도 모른다.

- The man <u>may</u> have been a beggar.
 (→It is possible that the man was a beggar.) 그 남자는 거지이었을 지도 모른다.

⊙ 가능성을 표현하므로 'May ~'형식으로 '기원'이나 'so that 주어 may ~ '형식으로 '목적-~하기 위하여' 등
을 나타낼 수 있다.

① '기원'- ' ~하소서'

- <u>May</u> you always be happy and healthy! 항상 행복하고 건강하소서!

② '주어 +동사 so that 주어 may ~ ' ~하기 위하여

- The students study math so that they <u>may</u> major in math.

그 학생들은 그들이 수학을 전공하기 위하여 수학을 전공한다.

🔍 확인문제 5

다음 문장에서 사용된 may의 용법의 허가인지 추측(추측)인지를 말하시오.

(01). I <u>may</u> be late, so don't wait for me.

(02). You <u>may</u> bring your cat back tomorrow.

(03). <u>May</u> we use your office for a few minutes?

(04). Visitors <u>may</u> use the room between 2 and 4 p.m.

(05). <u>May</u> we use your office for a few minutes?

(06). <u>May</u> I join your club activities?

(07). The student <u>may</u> be late for school.

《정답과 해설 26P》

Study 04 must

의무(=have to)	추측→ It is certain that 주어 +동사
～해야 한다.	～임에 틀림없다.

1. 의무: 'have to'로 바꿀 수 있다.

- Painters **must** work hard like oxen.
  (= Painters **have to** work hard like oxen.)   화가들은 황소처럼 열심히 작업을 해야 한다.
- We **must** protect our environment.
  (= We **have to** protect our environment.)   우리는 환경을 보호 해야만 한다.

2. 추측

현재추측	must 동사원형 ～(→It is certain that 주어+현재동사)
과거추측	must have p.p ～ (→ It is certain that 주어+과거동사)

(1). 현재추측: **must 동사원형 ～**(=It is certain that 주어+현재동사); ～임에 틀림없다.
  - He **must be** tired.
    (→It is certain that he is tired.)   그는 피곤함에 틀림없다.
  - You **must be** happy.
    (→ It is certain that you are happy.)   너는 행복함에 틀림없어.

(2). 과거추측: **must have p.p ～** (→ It is certain that 주어 +과거동사); ～이었음에 틀림없다.
  - She **must have been** tired.
    (→It is certain that he was tired.)   그녀는 피곤했음에 틀림없다.
  - The boys **must have been** brave.
    (→It is certain that the boys were brave.)   그 소년들은 용감했음에 틀림없다.

확인문제 6

다음 문장에서 사용된 must가 의무로 쓰였는지 추측으로 쓰였는지를 말하시오. 그리고 해석하시오.

(01). You must not forget to say "thank you."
(/   )

(02). Anne sings very well. She must be a singer.
(/   )

(03). You must get up early tomorrow morning.
(/   )

(04). Sarah must be a criminal of the robbery.
(/   )

(05). Genie must have been sick last week.
(/   )

(06). His car must be very expensive.
(/   )

《정답과 해설 260》

확인문제 7

다음 문장에서 must를 have to로 바꿔 쓰고 해석하시오.

(01). You must be honest.
(/   )

(02). You must study hard today.
(/   )

(03). Youth must give up their seat for old people.
(/   )

(04). Children must eat organic food.
(/   )

(05). We must wait for the train.
(/   )

(06). Hyeonwoo must pass this exam.
(/   )

(07). The people must follow the law.
(/   )

《정답과 해설 261》

05 can

| 능력;~ 할 수 있다.(= be able to) | 허가(=may); ~해도 좋다. |

1. 능력: ~할 수 있다.

- I **can** swim across the lake.
  (→ I **am able to** swim across the lake.) 나는 수영하여 이 호수를 건널 수 있다.
- The novelist **can** write a best novel.
  (→ The novelist **is able to** write a best novel.) 그 소설가는 베스트셀러를 쓸 수 있다.

2. 허가: ~해도 좋다.

- You **can** use my phone.
  (→ You **may** use my phone.) 너는 나의 폰을 사용해도 좋아.
- **Can** I join the club?
  (→ **May** I join the club?) 내가 그 클럽에 참여해도 될까요?

CF can't

능력부정	추측
~ 할 수 없다	~ 일 리 없다

① 능력부정

I **can't** solve the problems for myself. 나는 그 문제들을 혼자서 해결 할 수가 없다.

② 추측 – 부정적 추측

현재추측	can't 동사원형~ (→It is impossible that 주어+현재동사) ~일 리 없다.
과거추측	can't have p.p~(→It is impossible that 주어+과거동사) ~ 이었을 리 없다.

a. 현재추측: can't 동사원형~ (→It is impossible that 주어+현재동사) ~일 리 없다.

The old man **can't be** a spy.

(=It is impossible that the old man is a spy.)   그 노인은 스파일 리 없다.

b. 과거추측: can't have p.p~(→It is impossible that 주어+과거동사) ~ 이었을 리 없다.

The old man **can't have been** a spy.

(→It is impossible that the old man was a spy.)   그 노인은 스파이였을 리 없다.

확인문제 8

다음 문장을 can이 '능력'과 '허가', 또 can't가 '능력의 부정'과 '부정적 추측'인지를 각각 말하고 해석하시오.

(01). Can I speak to Brian?
(/   )

(02). How can I do that?
(/   )

(03). You can get some rest.
(/   )

(04). You can't be foolish.
(/   )

(05). Mary can't pass the entrance exam.
(/   )

(06). Can I go out and play baseball with Taeho?
(/   )

(07). You can say to your server, "May I have a glass of water?"
(/   )

(08). Only confident people can accept their mistakes.
(/   )

Study 06 shoud

'~ 해야 한다' 당연함을 나타낸다.

- We should recycle paper.
- You should take a short shower.
- Students should listen to their teachers.

우리는 종이를 재활용해야 한다.
너는 짧게 샤워해야 한다.
학생들은 선생님 말씀을 경청해야 한다.

🔍 확인문제 9

다음 문장을 해석하시오.

(01). Students should come to school on time.

　　　(　　　　　　　　　　　　　　　　　　　)

(02). You should not eat snacks during class.

　　　(　　　　　　　　　　　　　　　　　　　)

(03). We should try to stop global warming.

　　　(　　　　　　　　　　　　　　　　　　　)

(04). Climbers should try to make less trash.

　　　(　　　　　　　　　　　　　　　　　　　)

(05). You should recycle the plastic and bottles.

　　　(　　　　　　　　　　　　　　　　　　　)

(06). You should remember these special days.

　　　(　　　　　　　　　　　　　　　　　　　)

《정답과 해설 26P》

다음 문장을 should와 괄호안의 단어를 사용하여 영작하시오.

(01). 너는 물을 소중하게 여겨야 한다.(value)

( )

(02). 우리는 에너지를 절약해야 한다.(save)

( )

(03). 아이들은 종이를 낭비해서는 안 된다. (waste)

( )

(04). 우리는 나무를 베어서는 안 된다.(cut)

( )

(05). 너는 전등을 꺼야 한다. (turn off)

( )

CF 부정문을 만들 때는 반드시 조동사 다음에 not을 쓴다

You may **not** eat this candy. 너는 이 캔디를 먹을 수 없다.

You should **not** eat fast food. 너는 패스트푸드를 먹지 않아야 한다.

We should **not** sleep during class. 우리는 수업 중에 잠을 자면 안 된다.

The customer must **not** pay the bill. 그 고객이 그 청구서에 지불하면 안 된다.

You must **not** forget to remind me of it.

너는 나에게 그것을 상기시키는 것을 잊어서는 안 된다.

Kids under 7 need **not** pay to take the bus.

7세 이하의 아이들은 버스를 타기 위하여 지불할 필요 없다.

Study 07 used to

used to 동사원형	be used to 동사원형	be used to 동사원형ing
~하곤 했다	~하기 위하여 사용되다	~에 익숙하다

1. used to 동사원형: (과거에) ~하곤 했다. ~ 했었다.

- The boys used to go to the shore.
- He used to play the piano at night.
- The old man used to live in the cottage.

그 소년들은 해변에 가곤 했다.
그는 피아노를 연주하곤 했다.
그 노인은 오두막에서 살았었다.

2. be used to 동사원형: ~하기 위하여 사용되다.

- This bottle is used to contain water.
- Medical herbs are used to heal the patients.

이병은 물을 담기 위하여 사용된다.
약초들이 환자를 치료하기 위하여 사용된다.

3. be used to 동사원형ing: ~에 익숙하다.

- My son is used to getting up early.
- My grandmother is not used to driving a car.
- The boys are used to climbing mountains.

나의 아들은 일찍 일어나는 것에 익숙하다.
나의 할머니는 차를 운전하는데 익숙하지 않다.
그 소년들은 산에 오르는데 익숙하다.

확인문제 11

다음 문장을 각각 해석하시오.

(01). The girls used to run and play in the playground.

( )

(02). This textbook is used to teach English to children.

( )

(03). The people were used to living in the country.

( )

(04). The farmer used to sow flower seed in summer.

( )

(05). This tool was used to reap rice in the field.

( )

《정답과 해설 27P》

확인문제 12

다음 문장에서 틀린 부분을 찾아 올바로 고치세요. 그리고 해석하세요.

(01). We are used to swim in the Han river.

→ _____

( )

(02). Bulls were used to plowing the land in the 1970s.

→ _____

( )

(03). The foreigners used to speaking Korean.

→ _____

( )

(04). My father is not used to deal with a smart phone.

→ _____

( )

(05). They are used to pick up shells in the sea shore in our early days.

→ _____

( )

《정답과 해설 28P》

CF 과거를 표현하는 조동사+have p.p

may, must, can't, should, need 다음에 'have+p.p'가 와서 과거에 대한 내용을 나타낼 수 있다.

① may have p.p (과거에) ~이었을 지도 모른다.
- The man may have been a thief.　　　　그 남자는 도둑놈이었을 지도 모른다.

② must have p.p(과거에)~ 이었음에 틀림없다.
- The woman must have been a robber.　　그 여자는 강도였음에 틀림없다.

③ can't have been (과거에)~이었을 리 없다.
- The boy can't have been the man's son.　그 소년은 그 남자의 아들이었을 리 없다.

④ should have p.p (과거에) ~했어야만 했는데(안했다).
- You should have gone to the party.　　(과거에) 너는 파티에 갔어야만 했는데.

⑤ need have p.p (과거에) ~할 필요가 없었는데(했다).
- We need have bought the book.　　　　우리는 그 책을 살 필요가 없었는데.

확인문제 13

다음 문장을 각각 해석하시오.

(01). The man may have been a spy.
　　(　　　　　　　　　　　　　　　　　)

(02). The woman must have been a liar.
　　(　　　　　　　　　　　　　　　　　)

(03). The teacher can't have been a genius.
　　(　　　　　　　　　　　　　　　　　)

(04). You should have studied hard last night.
　　(　　　　　　　　　　　　　　　　　)

(05). You need not have borrowed the books.
　　(　　　　　　　　　　　　　　　　　)

《정답과 해설 27P》

Grammar in Reading

〈정답과 해설 20쪽〉

1. 다음 대화를 읽고 물음에 답하시오.

Taylor: You ⓐ <u>must</u> be Minhee. Do you remember me?
Minhee: Sure. How can I forget you, Taylor?
Taylor: Long time no see.
Minhee: We are used to play badminton together on weekends.
Taylor: Yes. We also went skating in winter. We had a lot of fun.
Minhee: I'll never forget our elementary school years.

1. 위 대화의 밑줄 친 ⓐ must와 의미가 같은 것을 모두 고르시오.

01. We must eat breakfast.
02. You must not miss the class.
03. You must not swim in the river.
04. The boys must be lost in the forest.
05. You must not eat and drink here.
06. Mina must come back by 9 o'clock.
07. The kids must not pick up the flowers.
08. I must do my homework before dinner.
09. Anne sings very well. She must be a singer.
10. We must not waste our money on useless things.

2. 위의 글에서 어법상 맞지 않는 것을 찾아 올바로 고치시오.

《정답과 해설 27P》

2. 다음 대화를 읽고 물음에 답하시오.

Brian: Hello. ⓐ <u>May</u> I speak to Sujin?
Sujin: Speaking. Who's calling, please?
Brian: This is Brian.
Sujin: Oh, Brian. What's up?
Brian: I lost your book. I'm so sorry.
Sujin: Oh, no. How did you lost it?
Brian: I think I left it on the subway.
Sujin: Then, you have to call the Lost and Found at the subway station.
Brian: Okay, I will. I'm so sorry.

1. 다음 중 밑줄 친 부분의 의미가 ⓐ와 같은 것을 모두 고르시오.

01. You may come by 9 o'clock.
02. You may use my camera.
03. May I ask you a question?
04. The work may not be difficult.
05. You may go out and play tonight.
06. You may have this pen.
07. She may know the answer.
08. You may get a new calendar.
09. The boys may cross the streets in the green light.
10. You may raise your hand when you have some questions.

2. 위의 글에서 어법상 맞지 않는 것을 찾아 올바로 고치시오.

Grammar in Reading

《정답과 해설 27~28쪽》

3. 다음 글에서 어법상 맞지 않는 것을 모두 찾아 쓰시오.

Are you enjoying the trip? Here are some tips for your stay in the city. When you crosses the streets, you should waits for the green light. You should wear a helmet when you ride a bike. Also, you should asked for help when you get lost. Have a nice stay in our city!
Are you having a good time in our city? Here is some tips for your stay in the city. When it rain, you should use an umbrella. You should take a shower when you get dirty. When you get sick, you should see a doctor.

4. 다음 문장에서 어법상 맞지 않는 것을 모두 찾아 올바로 고치시오.

In the past, eye charts were used to checking people's eyesight. But these days a new device is being using instead. It shows how good one's eyesight is. This device sends more than 10,000 beams of light into one's eye to measure his or her eyesight. As those beams go into the eye, it measures how accurately the eye's lens bends the light. After 10 seconds, the device can show how good or bad one's eyesight is. With this technology, people not need look at an eye chart and say the numbers.

〈정답과 해설 28P〉

1. 다음 문장에서 어법상 어색한 부분을 찾아 바르게 고쳐 쓰시오.

01. We must ate breakfast.
→ _____

02. Yumi should eat not too much.
→ _____

03. You must miss not the class.
→ _____

04. Junsu should studies hard.
→ _____

05. Mina should to learn about other cultures.
→ _____

06. How can you opened social doors?
→ _____

07. Tom can sent a message for me.
→ _____

08. We must to recycle empty bottles.
→ _____

09. They could brought some books for my sister.
→ _____

10. You must go to bed now to get up early next morning.
→ _____

2. 다음 우리말과 같은 의미가 되도록 'must'와 괄호 안의 단어를 이용하여 빈칸에 알맞은 말을 쓰시오.

01. 우리는 우리의 환경을 보호하여야 한다.(protect)
=We _____ _____ our environment.

02. 그들은 여기에 주차를 하면 안 됩니다. (park)
= They _____ _____ _____ here.

03. 우리는 우리 수학 숙제를 해야 한다. (do, homework)
= We _____ _____ _____ _____.

04. 너는 수업시간동안에 먹지 않아야 한다. (eat)
= You _____ _____ _____ during the class.

05. 너는 내일 아침 일찍 일어나야 한다. (get, early)
= You _____ _____ _____ _____ tomorrow morning.

3. 아래 문장에서 각각 사용된 must가 의무로 쓰였는지 추측(~임에 틀림없다)로 쓰였는지를 구별하고 해석하시오.

01. His answer must be false.
[/   ]

02. We must make a cleaner earth.
[/   ]

03. The workers must be tired.
[/   ]

04. This smart phone must be mine.
[/   ]

05. He must have gone to the farewell party.
[/   ]

06. The students must write an essay.
[/   ]

07. The girl must be an orphan now.
[/   ]

08. You must be on time for class.
[/   ]

09. The hikers must take their trash back home.
[/   ]

10. We must use less cars and plant many trees.
[/   ]

4. 다음 우리말과 같은 의미가 되도록 'may'와 괄호 안의 단어를 이용하여 빈칸에 알맞은 말을 쓰시오.

01. 너는 나의 연필을 사용해도 좋아.
→ _____

02. 너의 친구들이 이 캔디를 먹어도 좋아.
→ _____

03. 그녀가 나의 컴퓨터를 사용해도 좋아.
→ _____

04. 너는 나의 휴대폰을 빌릴 수 있어.(borrow, cell phone)
→ _____

05. James가 나의 생일파티에 와도 좋아.
→ _____

06. 그 남자는 스파이일지도 모른다.
→ _____

《정답과 해설 23P》

07. 너는 내일까지 그 리포트를 가져와도 돼.

→ _____

08. 너는 너의 차를 이 주차장에 주차해도 좋아.(park, parking lot)

→ _____

5. 다음 문장의 밑줄 친 may 추측과 허가 중 어떤 의미로 쓰였는지 구분하여 괄호 안에 쓰시오.

01. May I help you?

[/   ]

02. Tom may not be sick.

[/   ]

03. His answer may be false.

[/   ]

04. The employees may be tired.

[/   ]

05. May I touch your puppy?

[/   ]

06. Hello, may I speak to Sue?

[/   ]

07. You may use this phone.

[/   ]

08. You may go home now.

[/   ]

09. You may not ride a bike here.

[/   ]

10. May I play computer games now?

[/   ]

memo.

Chapter

08

Comparison
비교

Study 01 비교급과 최상급 형태

비교급을 만드는 방법에는 -er/-est를 붙이는 방법과 단어 앞에 more/most를 붙이는 방법, 불규칙적으로 변화하는 방법 등 있다. 일반적으로 1음절 단어는 -er/-est, 3음절 이상 단어는 more/most를 붙인다. 2음절의 경우 단어 끝이 -ow/-er/-y/-ly/-some 으로 끝나면 -er/-est를 붙이고 나머지 2음절어는 more/most를 붙인다. good/well 등은 불규칙적으로 변화한다.

-er/-est	more/most	불규칙변화형
1음절어와 2음절어중 -ow/-er/-y/-ly/-some으로 끝나는 단어	3음절 이상단어와 2음절 단어 중 -ow/-er/-y/-ly/-some를 제외한 단어	good/well bad/ill far old many/much 등

1. –er/–est만드는 방법

아래 주의해야 할 경우를 제외한 대부분의 1음절단어와 2음절 단어중 –ow/–er/–y/–ly로 끝나는 경우	–er/–est	high –higher –highest young –younger– youngest mild –milder –mildest warm– warmer– warmest cold –colder –coldest narrow–narrower–narrowest
주 의 해 야 할 경 우	–e로 끝나는 경우 –r과 –st만을 쓴다.	huge– huger –hugest brave– braver –bravest safe –safer –safest
	단모음+단자음으로 끝나는 경우: 마지막 자음을 하나 겹치고 –er, –est를 붙인다.	hot –hotter– hottest fat– fatter– fattest wet– wetter– wettest
	자음+ y로 끝나는 경우: y를 i로 고치고 –er/–est를 붙인다.	shy–shier–shiest easy– easier– easiest early– earlier– earliest ugly –uglier –ugliest noisy –noisier –noisiest funny –funnier –funniest merry–merrier–merriest chewy–chewier–chewiest

확인문제 1

다음 원급단어의 비교급, 최상급을 쓰시오.

(01). smart   _____, _____

(02). thin   _____, _____

(03). fat   _____, _____

(04). low _____, _____

(05). near _____, _____

(06). funny _____, _____

(07). long _____, _____

(08). bright _____, _____

(09). dark _____, _____

(10). fine _____, _____

(11). short _____, _____

(12). deep _____, _____

(13). young _____, _____

(14). weak _____, _____

(15). high _____, _____

(16). warm _____, _____

(17). cheap _____, _____

(18). cool _____, _____

(19). shy _____, _____

(20). heavy _____, _____

2. more/most 붙이는 방법

⊙ 2음절어 중 -ow, -er, -y, -ly로 끝나지 않은 단어

- polite 정중한 - more polite - most polite
- useful 유용한 - more useful - most useful
- selfish 이기적인 - more selfish - most selfish
- foolish 어리석은 - more foolish - most foolish
- active 활동적인 - more active - most active
- famous 유명한 - more famous - most famous
- honest 정직한 - more honest - most honest
- cheerful 유쾌한 - more cheerful - most cheerful
- patient 인내심 있는 - more patient - most patient
- sociable 사교적인 - more sociable - most sociable
- careful 주의 깊은 - more careful - most careful
- earnest 열렬한 - more earnest - most earnest

CF   2음절어 중 -ow, -er, -y, ly로 끝나는 단어는 -er/-est를 붙여서 비교급과 최상급을 만든다.

- witty 위트 있는 - wittier- wittiest
- fussy 까다로운 - fussier - fussiest
- early 이른 - earlier - earliest
- clever 영리한 - cleverer - cleverest
- greedy 탐욕스러운 - greedier - greediest
- narrow 좁은 - narrower - narrowest

⊙ 3음절 이상 단어

- diligent 근면한 - more diligent - most diligent
- difficult 어려운 - more difficult - most difficult
- popular 인기 있는 - more popular - most popular
- essential 필수적인 - more essential - most essential
- excellent 뛰어난 - more excellent - most excellent
- important 중요한 - more important - most important
- generous 관대한 - more generous - most generous
- humorous 유머러스한 - more humorous - most humorous
- optimistic 낙천적인 - more optimistic - most optimistic
- considerate 사려 깊은 - more considerate - most considerate

다음 각각 원급단어의 비교급과 최상급을 쓰시오.

(01). foolish _____, _____

(02). stupid _____, _____

(03). excellent _____, _____

(04). difficult _____, _____

(05). exciting _____, _____

(06). useful _____, _____

(07). important _____, _____

(08). honest _____, _____

(09). easy _____, _____

(10). famous _____, _____

3. 불규칙 변화형

• good/well	– better	– best
• bad/ill	– worse	– worst
• far ┌ (거리)	– farther	– farthest
└ (정도)	– further	– furthest
• late ┌ (시간)	– later	– latest
└ (순서)	– latter	– last
• old ┌ (나이)	– older	– oldest
└ (손위)	– elder	– eldest
• many/much	– more	– most
• little	– less	– least

확인문제 3

다음 각각의 원급단어의 비교급과 최상급을 쓰시오.

(01). many/much _____, _____

(02). good/well _____, _____

(03). bad/ill _____, _____

(04). little _____, _____

(05). late (순서) _____, _____ (시간) _____, _____

(06). old (손위) _____, _____ (나이) _____, _____

(07). far (정도) _____, _____ (거리) _____, _____

〈정답과 해설 29P〉

Study 02 비교의 방법

원급 비교	비교급 비교	최상급 비교

1. 원급 비교

– as ~ as

↔ not as(=so) ~ as

• A lily is as beautiful as a rose.

   ↔ A lily is not as(=so) beautiful as a rose.

백합은 장미만큼 아름답다.

백합은 장미만큼 아름답지 않다.

확인문제 4

다음 각 문장에서 (　　　) 안에 들어갈 알맞은 말을 쓰고 해석해보시오.

(01). Gogh is (　　　) old as your sister.

   → _____

(02). The politician is as famous (　　　) a popular singer.

   → _____

(03). Her voice is as sweet (　　　) your voice.

   → _____

(04). Her brother is not (　　　) kind as my brother.

   → _____

(05). Denise speaks English (　　　) well as Elizabeth.

   → _____

2. 비교급 비교

$$- \text{-er/ more} \sim \text{than}$$
$$\leftrightarrow \underline{\text{not -er/ more} \sim \text{than}}$$
$$= \text{less}$$

- A lily is more beautiful than a rose.　　　　　　　백합은 장미보다 더 아름답다.
  - ↔ A lily is not more beautiful than a rose.　　백합은 장미보다 아름답지 않다.
    - = A lily is less beautiful than a rose.
- Forgiveness is better than revenge.　　　　　　용서는 복수보다 낫다.
- The Amazon river is longer than the Nile river.　아마존 강은 나일강 보다 길다.
- Burj Khalifa in Dubai is higher than Skytree in Tokyo, Japan.

　　　　　　　　두바이에 있는 부리칼리파는 일본 동경에 있는 Skytree보다 더 높다.

🔍 확인문제 5

다음 괄호 안에 주어진 단어를 이용하여 비교급 문장을 완성하시오.

(01).The train is _____ the car. (fast)

(02). Science is _____ math. (interesting)

(03). Health is _____ money. (important)

(04). Bananas is _____ apples. (cheap)

(05). It is _____ before. (bright)

(06). Sally is _____ her sister. (careful)

(07). I am _____ Minho. (young)

(08). The movie was _____ the play. (interesting)

(09). Your garden is _____ Mr. Kim's. (beautiful)

(10). I work _____ Miss Ford. (quickly)

《정답과 해설 29P》

3. 최상급 비교

– the 최상급 (명사) of 복수 명사
– the 최상급 (명사) in (집단)단수명사

- Jack is the tallest of the three children.   Jack은 세 아이들 중에서 가장 크다.
- Jack is the tallest player in the team.   Jack은 그 팀에서 가장 큰 선수이다.

확인문제 6

다음 괄호 안의 단어를 사용하여 최상급 문장을 완성 하시오.

(01). John is _____ boy of all.(smart)

(02). Seoul is _____ city in Korea.(large)

(03). That room is _____ in this house. (bright)

(04). Today is _____ day of the year. (cold)

(05). Your bag is _____ of them all. (heavy)

(06). Today was _____ day of her life. (happy)

(07). Who is _____ actress in Korea? (famous)

(08). It is _____ car in the shop.(expensive)

(09). A queen bee is _____ of all the bees. (big)

(10). The man is _____ person in the group. (important)

《정답과 해설 29P》

Study 03 최상급에 해당하는 표현들

- ~ the -est in 단수명사
  = ~ the -est of 복수명사
  = 부정주어 ~ as(so) 원급 as
  = 부정주어 ~ 비교급 than
  = as ~ as any other 단수명사
  = 비교급 than any other 단수명사
  = 비교급 than all the other 복수명사
  = 비교급 than anyone else / anything else

• Tom is the cleverest in our class.

Tom은 우리학급에서 가장 영리하다.

= Tom is the cleverest of our classmates in our class.

Tom은 우리학급의 학급학생들 중에서 가장 영리하다.

= No other student is as(=so) clever as Tom in our class.

어떤 다른 학생도 우리학급에서 Tom 만큼 영리하지 않다.

= No other student is cleverer than Tom in our class.

어떤 다른 학생도 우리학급에서 Tom보다 더 영리하지 않다.

= Tom is as clever as any other student in our class.

Tom은 우리학급에서 어떤 다른 학생만큼 영리하다.

= Tom is cleverer than any other student in our class.

Tom은 우리학급에서 모든 다른 어떤 학생보다 더 영리하다.

= Tom is cleverer than all the other students in our class.

Tom은 우리학급에서 모든 다른 학생들보다 더 영리하다.

• Dan is the kindest in our village.

Dan은 우리 마을에서 가장 친절하다.

= Dan is the kindest of our friends in our village.

Dan은 우리 마을의 우리 친구들 중에서 가장 친절하다.

= No other friend is as kind as Dan in our village.

어떤 다른 친구도 우리마을에서 Dan만큼 친절하지 않다.

= No other friend is kinder than Dan in our village.

어떤 다른 친구도 우리 마을에서 Dan보다 더 친절하지 않다.

= Dan is as kind as any other friend in our village.

Dan은 우리 학급에서 다른 어느 친구만큼 친절하다.

= Dan is kinder than any other friend in our village.

Dan은 우리 마을에서 어떤 다른 친구 보다 더 친절하지 않다.

= Dan is kinder than all the other friends in our village.

Dan은 우리 마을에서 모든 다른 친구들 보다 더 친절하지 않다.

⊙ 'Dubai에 있는 Burj Khalifa는 세계에서 가장 높은 빌딩이다.'의 표현들

• Burj Khalifa in Dubai is the highest building in the world.

두바이 부리칼리파는 세계에서 가장 높은 빌딩이다.

= Burj Khalifa in Dubai is the highest building of all the buildings in the world.

두바이 부리칼리파는 세계에 있는 모든 빌딩들 중 가장 높은 빌딩이다.

= No other building in the world is higher than Burj Khalifa in Dubai.

세계의 어떤 다른 빌딩도 두바이 부리칼리파보다 더 높지 않다.

= No other building in the world is as high as Burj Khalifa in Dubai.

세계의 어떤 다른 빌딩도 두바이 부리칼리파만큼 높지 않다.

= Burj Khalifa in Dubai is as high as any other building in the world.

두바이 부리칼리파는 세계의 어떤 다른 빌딩만큼 높다.

= Burj Khalifa in Dubai is higher than any other building in the world.

두바이 부리칼리파는 세계의 어떤.다른 빌딩보다 더 높다.

= Burj Khalifa in Dubai is higher than all the other buildings in the world.

두바이 부리칼리파는 세계의 모든 다른 빌딩보다 더 높다.

= Burj Khalifa in Dubai is higher than anything else in the world.

두바이의 Burj Khalifa는 세계의 그 밖의 어떤 것 보다 더 높다.

🔍 확인문제 7

'ShimotsuiSeto는 세계에서 가장 긴 다리다.'에 해당하는 여러 표현들을 쓰시오.

(01). (최상급) :

    →

(02). (최상급) :

    →

(03). (원급) :

    →

(04). (비교급) :

    →

(05). (비교급) :

    →

(06). (비교급) :

    →

(07). No other bridge

    →

(08). No other bridge

    →

《정답과 해설 29P》

A. 비교급 강조;

훨씬– far, by far, still, even, a lot, much 하지만 very는 쓸 수 없다.

Seoul has far(= by far, still, even, a lot, much) more population than Busan.
서울이 부산보다 훨씬 많은 인구를 가지고 있다.

확인문제 8

다음 각 문장에서 어법상 맞지 않는 것을 찾아 올바로 고치시오. 그리고 각각 해석하시오.

(01). Jenny is very thinner than Tom.

→ _____

(02). Your computer is even slower than mine.

→ _____

(03). Mike looks a little older than his older brother.

→ _____

(04). This house is still worse than I thought.

→ _____

(05). Dooly is a lot more famous than Doner.

→ _____

(06). Your smart phone is very faster than hers.

→ _____

(07). Health is far more important than money.

→ _____

(08). This actor is still more popular than his father.

→ _____

(09). The girl is smart than her brother in the school.

→ _____

(10). The red bag is many more expensive than the black one.

→ _____

B. The 비교급, the 비교급 ; ～하면 할 수 록 ～하다.

The more we know, the more polite we are.
우리가 많이 알면 알수록 더 겸손해진다.

The more you read, the smarter you will become.
네가 많이 읽으면 읽을수록 더 영리해 진다.

확인문제 9

다음 각각의 문장을 해석해보시오.

(01). The more you have, the more you want.

→ _____

(02). The younger you are, the more quickly you can learn,

→ _____

(03). The harder you study, the better grades you will get.

→ _____

(04). The more expensive the food is, the better the service is.

→ _____

(05). The more you sleep, the more you will sleep.

→ _____

(06). The earlier we leave, the sooner we will arrive.

→ _____

(07). The harder you try, the more confidence you'll get.

→ _____

(08). The higher you go up the mountain, the colder it becomes.

→ _____

(09). The bigger the car is, the more fuel it uses.

→ _____

(10). The older we grew, the closer we became to each other.

→ _____

《정답과 해설 30P》

《정답과 해설 30P》

다음 문장에서 어법상 잘못된 문장을 올바로 쓰시오.

1.

Today's Yoga

First sit up straight on the mat and bend your knees out to the sides. Next, place your feet together and put your feet to your body as closer as possible. Hold your feet with your hands. Relax your body. Now breathe in and out slowly.

→ ＿＿＿＿＿＿＿＿를 ＿＿＿＿＿＿＿＿으로

2.

Do you have a piano at home? Its sounds are made when small hammers hit strings. The strings are inside the piano. On the outside of the piano, there are 52 white and 36 black keys. The white ones are long. The black ones, however, are shorter. They are also raised high than the white ones.

* key : (피아노)건반.

→ ＿＿＿＿＿＿＿＿를 ＿＿＿＿＿＿＿＿으로

Grammar in Reading

〈정답과 해설 30~31P〉

3.

Long ago, people who lived in caves made fires. They used fires to keep warm. At night they used them for light and found that they could see better with fires on. They also learned that wild animals like lions and tigers were afraid of fire. They were safe as longer as they had a fire on.

→ _____를 _____으로

4.

An earthquake can happen anytime anywhere in the world. In 1999, two large earthquakes hit Turkey and Taiwan, destroying large cities and killing thousands of people. These earthquakes were not actually the larger ones in history. Why were so many people killed in them? I strongly believe the answer is 'poor building construction'.

→ _____를 _____으로

5.

Good morning, everyone. I'm your tour guide for today. First, we are going to visit Changdeok Palace. It is one of the most famous palace in Seoul. For lunch, we are going to go to a Korean restaurant. You can enjoy Korean traditional food there. And then we will visit Namsan Hanok Village. There we will watch Korean mask dances and look around at old houses. You will have great fun today.

→ _____를 _____으로

〈정답과 해설 31P〉

1. '아마존 강은 세계에서 가장 긴 강이다.' 표현 들을 써보시오.

01. (최상급):

　→ _____

02. (최상급):

　→ _____

03. (원급):

　→ _____

04. (비교급):

　→ _____

05. (비교급):

　→ _____

06. (비교급):

　→ _____

07. No other river

　→ _____

08. No other river

　→ _____

〈정답과 해설 41P〉

2. 다음 <보기>와 같이 괄호 안의 단어와 'as ~as' '-er/more/less ~than' 등의 구문을 사용하여
두 문장을 한 문장으로 연결하시오.

> • Carlos is 168cm tall.
>   Wanda is 168cm tall, too.
>   → **Carlos is as tall as Wanda. (tall)**
>
> • This house is a large size.
>   That one is an X-large size.
>   → **This house isn't as(so) large as that one. (large)**
>   = **This house isn't larger than that one.**

01. The soldier is 13 years old. Michael is 14 years old.
    → The soldier _____ Michael. (old)
    or The soldier _____ Michael. (old)

02. This shirt is 30 dollars. That one is 30 dollars, too.
    → This shirt _____ that one. (expensive)

03. Your elder brother's height is 144cm. Your height is 149cm.
    → Your elder brother's height _____ yours. (tall)
    or Your elder brother's height _____ yours. (tall)

04. This building is ten stories high. That building is ten stories high, too.
    → This building _____ that building. (high)

05. My dad's weight is 76 kg. Your weight is 65 kg.
    → My dad's weight _____ yours.(heavy)

06. KTX can go 305 km/h. ITX can go 180km/h.
    → KTX _____ ITX. (fast)

07. This book is 6cm thick. That one is 8cm thick.
    → This book _____ that one. (thick)
    or This book _____ that one. (thick)

〈정답과 해설 31P〉

08. Mom is 45 years old. Dad is 45 years old.

→ Mom is _____ Dad.

3. 주어진 단어들을 사용하여 'as ~ as' 문장을 만드시오.

01. (Bill, rich, Susan)

→ _____

02. (his computer, new, mine)

→ _____

03. (my father, busy, a bee)

→ _____

04. (she, famous, a movie star)

→ _____

4. 다음 대화를 읽고, 괄호 안의 단어를 알맞은 형태로 바꾸어 'as ~ as' 구문을 완성하시오.

01. Tony: I'm 15 years old.
    Becky: I'm 15 years old, too.
    → Tony is _____ Becky. (old)

02. Tony: My bag was 30,000 won.
    Becky: My bag was 40,000 won.
    → Tony's bag was _____ Becky's. (expensive)

5. 다음 우리말과 같은 뜻이 되도록 괄호 안의 단어를 이용하여 원급 비교 문장을 완성하시오.

01. 과학은 역사만큼이나 흥미롭다.
    = Science is _____ history. (interesting)

02. 개는 고양이만큼이나 영리하다.
    = A dog is _____ a cat. (clever)

03. 내 목소리는 네 목소리만큼 크지 않다.
    = My voice is _____ yours. (loud)

6. 두 문장의 의미가 같도록 'as ~ as' 구문을 사용하여 빈칸을 완성하시오.

01. Arnold studies harder than Nora.
    = Nora doesn't study _____ Arnold.

02. Ralphie is taller than Phoebe.
    = Phoebe _____ Ralphie.

03. My son likes baseball more than basketball.
    = My son _____ baseball.

04. Math is more difficult than science for me.
    = Science _____ math for me.

05. A banana is more popular than a kiwi.
    = A kiwi _____ a banana.

7. 다음 표를 보고 as ~ as를 이용하여 세 사람을 비교하는 문장을 3문장으로 쓰시오.

Name	Weight	Height
Snowball	68kg	178m
Jones	46kg	178cm
Napoleon	46kg	168cm

01. _____

02. _____

03. _____

8. 다음 표의 내용과 일치하도록, 괄호에 주어진 단어를 사용하여 문장을 완성하시오.

	Jones	David	Mike	John
height (키)	177cm	177cm	175m	180cm
playing tennis (1주일 간)	3회	3회	매일	2회

01. Jones _____ David. (tall)

02. John _____ among them. (tall)

03. David _____ Mike. (tennis, often)

9. 다음 수준별 선택형 3개 중 각각을 as ~ as 형식으로 보기와 같이 적절한 문장을 쓰시오.

	Snowball	Napoleon
선택1	I'm 15 years old.	I'm 15 years old.
선택2	I can jump high.	I can jump high.
선택3	I don't love sports.	I love sports.

보기 : • Snowball is as pretty as Napoleon.

01. _____

02. _____

03. _____

〈정답과 해설 32P〉

10. 아래 표는 세 개의 강을 비교한 표입니다. <보기>의 문법구조만을 사용하여 문장을 만드시오.

	*Length(km)	*Width(km)	*Depth(m)
River A	7,000	10	60
River B	5,500	5	50
River C	7,000	7	55

* Length: 길이, Width: 넓이, Depth: 깊이

보기:

• Rules for 'as ~ as' comparison

Rule 1. as ~ as 비교

e.g. Alice is as beautiful as Mary.

Rule 2. 배수 as ~ as

e.g. This is three times as great as that.

Rule 3. 부정주어 (nobody, nothing 등) ~

e.g. Nobody sings as well as she does.

01. Rule 1을 사용

→ River A _____

02. Rule 2을 사용

→ River A _____

03. Rule 3을 사용

→ Nothing _____

《정답과 해설 32P》

11. 다음 문장 중 어법상 잘못된 것을 찾아 올바로 고치시오.

01. That building is more higher than this building.

02. This butterfly is big than that one.

03. Time is important than money.

04. This bag is the most prettiest of all.

05. Dad had least money than mom.

06. The girl is as tall than the boy.

07. A pink case is as bigger as two red ones.

08. The yellow logo is not as good than the brown one.

09. Baseball is one of the more popular sports.

10. Jeniffer Lee is as beautiful as her sister.

11. We had much rain this year than last year.

12. He was as more poor as a church mouse.

13. Anything is so precious as time.

14. Stuart is stronger than all the other boy in his class.

15. Ann has many books than his sister has.

memo.

저자 손 창연 선생님 강의 수강 후기들!!

김♥규
손창연쌤의영어문법!!
아 정말 손창연선생님은 대단하신 것 같네요. 체계적인 문법과 암기 방법 그리고 모르는 문제에 대한 상세한 설명까지.. 거기에다 또 사회적 이슈까지 알려주어서 배경지식을 팍팍!! 정말 책에 나온 것처럼 독자들에게 정의에 편에 서는 용기와 영감도 주시네요.

박♥우
선생님의 체계적인 수업 덕분에 저의 영어 실력이 많이 는 것 같습니다. 핵심적인 내용들을 외우기 쉽게 해주셔서 여러 모로 도움이 많이 되었습니다. 그리고 선생님의 현실적인 문장들은 재미없는 문장들보다는 난 것 같네요.ㅎㅎ

권♥운
알기 쉽게 재미 있게 노래해주셔서 이해가 잘 되었습니다.

배♥은
내신 할 때만 단기로 외우고 잊어버렸던 문법이 손창연 선생님께서 쉽게 외우는 법과 여러가지 사회문제와 엮어 말씀해주신 덕에 더 쉽게 이해했습니다. 영작실력도 늘것 같고 문법도 감으로 찍던 문제가 줄 것 같습니다. 문법을 집중적으로 가르쳐준 학원은 없었는데 매일 지루하지 않고 핵심을 조리 있게 잘 설명해 주셔서 영어 실력이 향상 된 것 같습니다.

하♥준
영문법강의 Good!
처음에 실력있는 선생님 소개로 중학교 1학년 때 오게 된 손창연 논리영어학원은 저에게 영어문법의 기초를 잡을 수 있게 해준 학원입니다. 그래서 중학교1,2,3학년 학교내신 영어성적을 잘 받을 수 있었습니다. 저는 지금 고등학교 진학을 몇 달 남겨두지 않은 한 학생인데 모자랐던 영어과목을 채움으로써 좋은 자립형 사립고에 진학하게 되었습니다. 중학교를 끝내는 시점에서 영문법을 다시 한 번 정리하기 위하여 1년여 만에 다시 재원하고 있습니다.

이 학원에서는 뼈에 사무치는 영어문법, 영문법 제 1조, OEG시리즈 등의 좋은 문제들로 만들어진 책들을 손창연 원장님의 직강으로 수업을 들을 수 있고, 그로인해 영문법의 핵심을 파악해 문법문제는 물론이고, 영어 구조가 머릿속에 훤히 드러나서 독해, 영작 등의 문제들도 큰 자신감을 얻어 쉽게 풀 수 있었습니다

김♥우
저는 중국에 있는 국제학교에 다니는 중2 학생 입니다. 저는 뼈에 사무치는 영어문법을 손창연저자 선생님으로부터 배우면서 많은 도움을 받았습니다. 그리고 선생님이 시사이야기 등을 재미있게 하시면서 가르치셨기 때문에 머릿속에 잘 들어오고 문법에 대하여 한 발짝 더 나아간 것 같습니다. 문법을 배웠을 뿐인데 Essay을 쓰는 능력과 독해에 도움을 많이 받은 것 같습니다.

정♥윤
손창연 영어 문법 강의를 듣고 지루했던 영어문법이 조금 나아졌습니다. 더 이해도 하기 쉽고 암기도 빨리 되어서 기분이 좋습니다.

김♥준
전에는 중학교 내신도 안돼고 문법이 정말 외울 것 많고 어려웠는데 이 책으로 공부하니 노래로 외우기 쉽고 이해도 잘돼서 이제는 문법에 자신감이 납니다. 뼈사 파이팅!!

seeenglish.com

중학내신만점대비
영문법 쏙쏙·영어 쑥쑥

저자 손 창연 선생님 강의 수강 후기들!!

-홈페이지에 실명으로 올린 내용들이나 이름 가운데를 ♥처리 합니다.-

임♥민

항상 영어문법강의를 듣고 나면 졸리고 지루하고 너무나도 싫고, 무엇보다 배운 내용을 까먹었었는데 손창연 선생님께서는 어려워하는 부분을 잘, 반복적으로 해주셔서 너무 좋은 것 같습니다. 특히나, 외우기 어려운 부분들은 직접 만드신 책에 암기법을 만들어주셔서 외우기 정말 쉽습니다. 여태까지 문법강의를 여러번 들음에도 불구하고 항상 부족하고 기억도 못했는데 손창연 선생님이 하시는 문법강의는 개념을 콕콕 집어주시고 지루하지도 않아 너무 좋습니다.

황♥현

문법수업으로 에세이 쓰는데도 도움이 많이 되고 있습니다.

지금 두 번 째 주재원 생활 중인 중2 학생입니다. 6살 때 폴란드로 가서 4년, 그리고 12살 때 다시 브라질로 나와 3년째 거주중입니다. 제가 폴란드에서 문법을 제대로 배우지 않아서 브라질에서 공부하는데 많이 불편했습니다. 항상 에세이를 써도 내가 쓰고 있는게 맞는건지 틀린건지 몰라 항상 쓰고 지우고 다시 쓰고 지우고를 항상 반복했습니다. 그리고 항상 성적을 낮추는 것은 항상 문법이었습니다. 그래서 이번에 한국 들어 왔을 땐 어머니와 고민하여 문법을 공부해보기로 해서 이 학원으로 오게되었습니다. 이제 공부한지 2주차 되었는데 많이 늘었다는것을 공부하면서 느낄 수 있었습니다. 항상 힘들었던 에세이도 학원에서 매번 다른 주제로 써와서 그 다은 수업에선 그 에세이를 읽고 틀린 부분들을 찾아내고 고치고 해서 나의 문제점을 찾아낼 수 있었습니다. 계속 하다 보니 에세이를 쓸때도 다시 쓰는 경우도 줄어들고 쓰는 속도도 빨라졌습니다.
그리고 항상 감으로 그냥 찍어서 쓰던 문법들을, 맞는지 틀렸는지도 모르고 그냥 쓰던 문법들을, 논리적으로 왜 맞고 왜 틀렸는지를 구별해주니, 저는 저의 문법에 확신을 가지게 되었습니다.

신♥영

토플 수업보다 훨씬 알맹이 가득

저는 외국에서 재학중인 고등학교 1학년 학생입니다. 영어를 7살 때부터 배웠지만 아직까지도 문법이 미약해서 힘들고 있어요. 토플이랑 SAT, 등등 고등학생들에게 요구되는 너무 많은 과제량 시험들도 벅찬데 저에게 문법은 상당히 큰 고비였습니다. 그러다 우연히 손창연 논리 문법학원을 알게 되었어요.

매일 아침 9시에 나가 4시간동안 토플 수업을 듣고 있습니다. 늘 똑같은걸 들려주고, 읽혀주고, 씌어 주는것 밖에 하지 않는점에서 많이 불만이 컸어요. 무엇보다도 에세이를 쓸 때, 읽기 본문을 해석할때 역시 미약했던 문법이 문제가 되습니다. 17살이 되도록 수동태의 쓰임과 시제, 관사, 복수와 단수조차 햇갈리던 저는 손창연 선생님에게 그간 궁금했던 문법, 잘 몰랐던 점 모두 뻥 뚫리듯 해결되었습니다. 솔직히 아침에 가는 토플학원도, 지금까지 해오던 과외도 너무 지루했는데 이 학원만큼은 아, 배우고싶다. 라는 생각이 들었어요. 이 수업을 듣고서 저에게 당장 필요했던 토플 수업에도 많이 도움이 됩니다.

저는 이 학원을 일주일에 2번, 2시간씩 수업을 듣고 있습니다. 매일매일 오라고 시키는 다른 학원에 비해 시간이 적은 편이지만 2달의 방학기간을 한국에 와 수업 들으면서 가장 효과를 보고 있어요. 이제 2주~3주밖에 수업을 듣지 않았지만 제 머릿속에 기초문법과 활용까지 정리가 되어 2달동안 배우면 지금까지 햇갈려왔던 문법들을 효과적으로 쓸 수 있을것 같습니다.

손♥솔

중학교 때 부터 영어를 포기했던 나에게 손창연 선생님의 강의는 나에게 한줄기 빛이 될것만 같았다. 무조건 암기만 하라는 식의 강의가 아닌 원리를 가르쳐주고, 그 원리를 이용해서 영작까지 조금이나마 수월하게 만들어주셨다. 해석도 끊어 읽기의 구성단위가 눈에 보이면서 점점 쉽게 풀리기 시작해 고등학교의 긴 지문도 해석이 꼼꼼하게 잘 되는 것 같고 모의고사의 문법문제도 하나하나 따질 수 있게 되어 좋았다.

seeenglish.com